T0299571

The CBT
Anxiety Solution
WORKBOOK

A BREAKTHROUGH TREATMENT *for* OVERCOMING FEAR, WORRY & PANIC

MATTHEW MCKAY, PhD
MICHELLE SKEEN, PsyD
PATRICK FANNING

New Harbinger Publications, Inc.

Publisher's Note

This publication is designed to provide accurate and authoritative information in regard to the subject matter covered. It is sold with the understanding that the publisher is not engaged in rendering psychological, financial, legal, or other professional services. If expert assistance or counseling is needed, the services of a competent professional should be sought.

NEW HARBINGER PUBLICATIONS is a
registered trademark of New Harbinger Publications, Inc.

Distributed in Canada by Raincoast Books

Copyright © 2017 by Matthew McKay, Michelle Skeen, and Patrick Fanning
New Harbinger Publications, Inc.
5674 Shattuck Avenue
Oakland, CA 94609
www.newharbinger.com

Cover design by Amy Shoup

Acquired by Catharine Meyers

Edited by Susan LaCroix

Library of Congress Cataloging-in-Publication Data on file

24   23   22

10   9   8   7   6   5   4   3

Contents

1   The Anxiety Problem   1

2   The Alarm Response   5

3   Assessment   21

4   Motivation   31

5   Preparation   39

6   The Anxiety Solution   79

7   You Can Face Fear   101

8   Reducing Worry with Defusion   115

9   Correcting Your Anxiety Lens   127

10   Distress Tolerance Skills   145

11   Relapse Prevention   167

     Appendix I: Comprehensive Coping Inventory (CCI)   181

     Appendix II: Worksheets   185

     Appendix III: Depression Anxiety Stress Scales-21 (DASS-21)   207

     Appendix IV: Interoceptive Exposure   211

     Appendix V: Acceptance and Action Questionnaire (AAQ-II)   219

     References   221

CHAPTER 1

The Anxiety Problem

Fear is a natural and valuable emotion. It has great survival value for human beings, preparing us to fight for survival or run away quickly from a threat. But too much fear in the form of chronic anxiety is incredibly painful and debilitating.

Anxiety is prolonged fear that persists in the absence of a real threat: after a threat is over, during situations that aren't actually very dangerous, or before a potential threat in the future. When anxiety becomes chronic and dominates your life, it morphs into an anxiety disorder.

Research consistently shows that cognitive behavioral therapy (CBT) is the most effective anxiety treatment. It works better than drugs, psychoanalysis, hypnosis, and all the other ways we have tried to treat anxiety over the years.

Broadly speaking, two CBT approaches for treating anxiety have emerged: coping and exposure. Coping is changing how you think, evaluating threats more accurately, and building confidence in your ability to handle a threat so that you are gradually less afraid. Exposure is purposefully experiencing what you are afraid of, disproving your dire predictions of disaster, until your fear naturally subsides. The most recent data show that both approaches help, but exposure can work faster and results in larger, longer-lasting reductions in anxiety.

The first two-thirds of this book teach you everything you need to know to apply the latest and most effective protocol for exposure, called *inhibitory learning*. It was developed by a team of therapists and researchers (Craske, Treanor, Conway, Zbozinek, and Vervliet) who published their results in 2014. This special exposure process will help you overcome anxiety as rapidly and completely as possible.

This book also covers the most effective coping strategies used in CBT and related therapies: coping planning, defusion, cognitive flexibility, and distress tolerance. They are research-tested, highly effective techniques that will augment and strengthen your anxiety recovery program.

How to Use This Book

Using this book is simple: continue reading, working through the first six chapters in order. Do the exercises as you come to them, thoroughly and diligently, before going on to the next section or skipping ahead. Along the way, you may be advised to also work in chapters 7–10. Finally, read the final chapter on relapse prevention.

You are about to start a challenging but very rewarding journey. Here is a preview of the main attractions:

Chapter 2 goes into the details of the alarm response, how we perceive and appraise threats, the fight/flight reaction, and typical behavioral responses. It allows you to compare your symptoms to the six most commonly diagnosed anxiety disorders:

1. Generalized anxiety disorder

2. Social anxiety disorder

3. Obsessive-compulsive disorder

4. Panic disorder

5. Specific phobia

6. Post-traumatic stress disorder

You will begin making a list of feared situations that you will carry forward into future chapters. At the end of the chapter is an exercise to help you identify your particular fear response and begin to shape your treatment plan.

Chapter 3 is all about assessment. You will begin an inventory of your feared situations, your level of distress for each, and which of several safety behaviors you tend to use:

- Avoiding what's making you anxious

- Seeking reassurance from others

- Distraction

- Procrastination

- Checking and double-checking

- Overpreparing for stressful encounters

- Perfectionism

- Ritual thoughts or actions

- List making to avoid forgetting and uncertainty

- Using drugs or alcohol to take the edge off

By far the most common safety behavior is *avoidance*. The chapter concludes with a checklist to find out which types of avoidance you favor: avoiding certain situations, avoiding certain thoughts, or avoiding certain physical sensations.

Chapter 4 is where you will work to build motivation for facing your feared situations. You'll assess the costs of your avoidance and other safety behaviors in nine domains:

1. Friendships

2. Family

3. Parenting

4. Work/education

5. Self-care/health

6. Pleasure/recreation

7. Life goals

8. Service to others

9. Romantic relationships

You will also identify and rate your positive values in these domains and list the activities and accomplishments you have been missing because of chronic anxiety. Finally, you will consider the importance of willingness when facing situations you have been avoiding.

Chapter 5 is the planning chapter in which you will list various ways you plan to stop your safety behaviors and expose yourself to the situations, feelings, and thoughts you have been avoiding. For each of your planned exposures you will predict the worst possible outcome and set a percentage probability for the outcome happening as predicted. After consulting many detailed examples of inventories composed by people suffering from all the different anxiety disorders, you will arrive at the end of the chapter with your own detailed exposure inventory.

Chapter 6 guides you through the actual exposure process: when to do it, what to experience first, how to prepare for exposures, evaluating your results, how often to do exposures, and so on.

Chapter 7 is the first of the supplemental coping chapters. It explains how to increase your sense of efficacy by developing a coping plan for your worst-case scenario.

Chapter 8 teaches the cognitive skill of *defusion*, a technique for coping with fearful thoughts, adapted from acceptance and commitment therapy.

Chapter 9 corrects your anxiety lens by teaching you how to appraise threats more accurately.

Chapter 10 works on increasing your distress tolerance, using techniques from dialectical behavior therapy, such as mindfulness, self-soothing, and relaxation.

Chapter 11 guides you in crafting a plan for relapse prevention, so that you can deal with any anxiety that crops up in the future.

Appendices contain all the worksheets in one place for ease of photocopying, extra instructions for panic disorder, and some useful standard measures for mental health professionals to use.

CHAPTER 2

The Alarm Response

In this chapter you will learn about the alarm response to threats, identify your type of anxiety, and begin to plan your treatment.

Chronic anxiety is like having an alarm sound in your mind and body that won't turn off. It just keeps ringing and warning you of danger. Everyone has a hardwired alarm system designed for survival. It helps you survive by mobilizing you to deal with threats. To understand how this valuable alarm response gets stuck in the "On" position, we first have to see how the mechanism works. There are four steps in the alarm response:

1. *Perception of threat*—the alarm sounds.

2. *Appraisal of threat*—you assess how serious the danger is and whether you have the resources to cope.

3. *Physiological and emotional responses*—you experience a cascade of physical sensations preparing you to deal with danger, and the emotion of fear.

4. *Behavioral response*—you do something to feel safer, such as avoiding the threat, postponing the threat until later, distracting yourself from the threat, and so on.

Perception of Threat

There are three kinds of threats we are always alert for. The first is *external*. You're out in the woods and notice a bear lumbering in your direction. Or your boss frowns and says she's concerned about your performance. Or your partner seems withdrawn and disconnected. Whether the threat is physical injury, loss of your job and livelihood, or a possible rejection, the danger is that something bad will happen to you via outside forces.

Internal threats originate with sensations in your own body. Any kind of physical pain is an example of an internal threat. A surprising, unfamiliar sensation can be threatening, as are sensations associated with danger, such as rapid heartbeat, shortness of breath, or light-headedness.

The third type of threat is a *conditioned* threat, or phobia. This is an object, a situation, or even an internal experience that's not very dangerous itself, but has become associated with the *expectation of harm*. This process, based on classical conditioning, is how phobias are formed. Most of us experience very little sense of danger getting in a car. But if your car gets linked in your mind to a terrible accident you witnessed, or a scary near-collision you experienced, something may change. Your car changes from a neutral, non-frightening stimulus into a conditioned, threatening stimulus. You now have the same fearful response to driving your car as you had to the accident or scary near-collision.

When these learned linkages occur, almost anything can become a conditioned stimulus/ threat. You're probably aware of some of these phobias—heights, tight spaces, freeways, hypodermics, elevators, airplanes, public places, dizzy feelings, bees, feeling hot, darkness, thunder, rodents, dogs, spiders, and so on.

Appraisal of Threat

Once the alarm has gone off, your mind kicks in, trying to determine how much danger you face. First, there is an assessment of the *level of threat*. How big is the bear? Is it moving toward you? Does it look aggressive? In the case of conditioned threats (phobias) the evaluation of danger may be near instantaneous, and largely depends on how close you are to the feared object or situation.

Appraisal of the level of threat can run the gamut from accurate to utterly wrong. Your evaluations of conditioned threats, because they're driven by a learned relationship between a neutral stimulus and grave danger, will usually be distorted. Inaccurate or distorted assessments of danger are called *misappraisals*, and two components of the treatment program in this book will help you overcome them.

In addition to appraising the immediate threat, your mind will also try to predict outcomes. What bad things might happen in five minutes, tomorrow, in a month? This fortune-telling response to threat is natural. Assessing possible catastrophic outcomes has helped us survive as a species. But when your mind locks onto threats and won't let go, when you can't stop preparing for all the harmful things that could happen, a normal mental process has gone awry. Instead of protecting you, this *worry/rumination* response can drive anxiety to overwhelming levels. This treatment program includes a component called *defusion* that will help you deal with ruminative thoughts.

The third appraisal in response to threat is an assessment of your ability to cope. Do you feel strong enough to face it? Do you have the resources to withstand the pain or stress this threat might bring? The appraisal of your ability to cope, if it is high, leads to *self-efficacy*—confidence that you can deal with difficult things. If it is low, you may experience *distress intolerance*—a sense that you can be quickly overwhelmed by painful events. Distress intolerance is a major contributor to chronic anxiety, and there are two components of this treatment program that target it.

Here is an outline of the typical threat appraisal process, teased apart and slowed down so that you can clearly see the three types of appraisals that determine whether your response will be a decline in anxiety or escalating anxiety and avoidance:

Perception of Threat: The alarm sounds: Danger!

Appraisals:

1. Big Danger?

   No—Alarm stops, anxiety/arousal declines.

   Yes—Alarm continues: Danger!

2. Catastrophic possibilities?

   No—Alarm stops, anxiety/arousal declines.

   Yes—Alarm continues: Danger!

3. More than I can cope with?

   No—Alarm stops, anxiety/arousal declines.

   Yes—Alarm continues: Danger!

Notice that the alarm bell shuts off if your appraisal of the threat or future danger is low. Likewise, the alarm diminishes or stops if you determine that you have the coping resources to face the threat. Only if the current or future danger seems high *and* you lack the ability to cope does the alarm continue, triggering both anxiety/fear and physiological arousal.

Avoidance behaviors typically occur only *after* anxiety/fear and arousal have been triggered. The decision to avoid is often automatic and unconscious, unless you have a strong reason to face the threat (for example, avoidance would trigger dire negative consequences, or there is something you value about facing this particular fear). You will learn, in this treatment program, how to consciously and deliberately make the decision to face threats and the anxiety they trigger.

Physiological and Emotional Responses

The physiological response to threat has been labeled the *fight-or-flight* reaction (Cannon, 1915), and more recently the *fight, flight, freeze* reaction (Clark, 2011). As soon as you decide there is a significant threat, your body reacts with a rapid sequence of protective responses. Your sympathetic nervous system triggers the pituitary gland to produce the stress hormone ACTH, and your adrenal gland to release the neurotransmitter epinephrine. Ultimately this results in:

- a boost in blood pressure
- accelerated heart rate
- more rapid breathing
- slowing or stopping of digestion
- constriction of blood vessels in your skin (to minimize bleeding)
- dilation of blood vessels in your big muscles (to help you run or fight)
- dilation of pupils (to see better)
- tunnel vision
- shaking

All of these autonomic reactions prepare you to survive a threat in the best possible way by (1) running away, (2) fighting and defending yourself, or (3) freezing and playing dead. Your brain decides which of these to do in just a few seconds.

Meanwhile, as your body reacts, the hypothalamus and the limbic areas of your brain are beginning an emotional response—fear (a threat is right in front of you) or anxiety (a threat may occur sometime in the future). The emotion of fear/anxiety creates a painful level of arousal that makes you want to do something to stop it. While fear is adaptive, motivating you to avoid danger, false alarms trigger fear-driven avoidance that makes you run from what isn't dangerous.

Behavioral Responses

All emotions share a single function—to organize and motivate behavior that helps you survive. Anger, for example, drives aggressive behavior to protect you from attacks. Sadness pushes you to withdraw so you can reevaluate following a loss or failure. And fear urges you to resist or avoid whatever scares you. So embedded in every emotion is an innate, hardwired urge to take action that helps to keep us alive.

The urge triggered by fear or anxiety is to seek safety. The most common safety behavior is avoidance—the flight part of the fight-or-flight reaction. Avoidance can take three forms: avoiding certain situations, avoiding certain thoughts, or avoiding certain sensations. Or instead of immediate avoidance, you might try to determine whether you are safe by checking for danger or seeking reassurance to ascertain whether the threat is as dangerous as you feared. If a threat is unavoidable, you might perform certain mental or physical rituals like invoking divine help or hand washing to feel safer. Safety behaviors can take many forms.

• *Example: Sheila's Alarm Response*

Several hours after getting home from a baseball game where Sheila ate two ballpark franks, she started to have sharp stomach pain. The threat led to an immediate appraisal of the level of danger.

Sheila's mother had died of cancer several years before, and had endured a great deal of pain. As a result, Sheila had begun to recognize physical pain as something dangerous, something alarming. What would turn out to be a bad hot dog was *misappraised* as highly dangerous and perhaps life threatening.

Sheila began trying to predict the future. Perhaps this was cancer, and she'd need surgery and chemotherapy. Like her mother, she might not survive. How would she provide for her two teenage boys, given that her ex-husband was a lunatic and would damage her sons if he got his hands on them? How would she keep a roof over her head if she couldn't work anymore? Sheila worried, or *ruminated*, about cancer until she threw up. Because she'd had a number of stomach upsets lately, she started thinking that maybe she also had irritable bowel disease.

As she struggled with the weight of catastrophic possibilities, Sheila wondered how she would cope. Her mother had "given up" at the end, and maybe she would, too. Sheila suspected that the stress would be overwhelming and that she couldn't cope.

The misappraisal, worry/rumination, and distress intolerance were taking a toll. Sheila could feel her heart beginning to race. Her face and chest felt hot. She was light-headed. When she stood up, her legs felt shaky and weak. Now the alarm response began merging with growing anxiety. Both her body and her emotions were screaming "Danger!" Sheila noticed all this and thought, *I'm in real trouble.*

Half an hour later Sheila indulged in a common safety behavior—seeking reassurance. She went online to read about stomach and colon cancer as well as irritable bowel syndrome. Weeks later when a friend invited her to another ball game, Sheila turned her down, using the most common safety behavior—avoidance.

False Alarms

When you react with fear and safety behaviors like avoidance to low-danger objects or situations, that's a false alarm. The more false alarms you experience, the more you suffer unnecessary anxiety and arousal. Frequent false alarms result in avoiding things you don't need to avoid, constricting and diminishing your life.

False alarms have four causes:

- Habitual avoidance—responses to conditioned or other low-danger threats. Avoidance keeps you from learning that your conditioned threats aren't dangerous, that you can tolerate and cope with them, and that you don't have to run from them.

- Ruminating about future catastrophes—trying to predict and plan for every possible danger in order to avoid it.

- Misappraising the level of threat—deciding the danger is worse than it is.

- Distress intolerance—the belief that you can't stand or cope with threats or the anxiety they trigger.

These four factors not only create false alarms, but they also usually combine to *maintain* your anxiety disorder. They are literally driving and deepening your fear and your pain. Each of the treatment steps that follow in this book targets one or more of these factors. As you free yourself of their influence, your anxiety and fear, your arousal, and all the constrictions that avoidance has placed around your life will greatly diminish.

The Anxiety Disorders

In the *DSM-5*, the diagnostic manual followed by most therapists and used by health insurance companies to approve payment, there are six types of anxiety disorders: generalized anxiety disorder, social anxiety disorder, obsessive-compulsive disorder, panic disorder, specific phobia, and post-traumatic stress disorder. They are significantly different from each other, and yet there are key factors common to all. Some people's anxiety fits neatly into one diagnosis and some people's anxiety spans two or three categories.

Let's look at the criteria for each and which symptoms sound familiar to you. Put a check by each disorder that might apply to you, and list the situations that you fear.

☐ *Generalized Anxiety Disorder*

If you have generalized anxiety disorder (GAD), you worry about multiple things. You focus on all the bad things that might happen. Everyone worries at times about money, work, or relationships, but you worry too much and for too long. The excessive worrying prevents you from enjoying a full life. The core experience is an uncontrollable feeling of *uncertainty* and a fear of catastrophic outcomes. While worry is an attempt to overcome uncertainty by predicting and trying to prevent bad things that could happen, *it has the effect of making you more anxious and uncertain, not less.* As your anxiety rises, you then use *safety behaviors* to cope—things like checking, reassurance seeking, procrastinating, avoiding, overpreparing, using drugs and alcohol, distracting yourself, and other behaviors.

Generalized anxiety disorder symptoms include:

- restlessness

- fatigue

- difficulty concentrating

- irritability

- muscle tension

- sleep problems

- difficulty controlling worry

Situations I worry about: _____

_____

_____

☐ *Social Anxiety Disorder*

As someone who struggles with social anxiety, you fear rejection and social shame. You worry excessively about what others may think of you. You might avoid jobs or social situations that would put you in the position of being judged by others and potentially criticized or rejected. To regulate these feelings of anxiety you may tend to isolate, leaving you feeling lonely and limiting your life and relationships.

Social anxiety disorder symptoms can include:

- feeling highly anxious around people and experiencing difficulty talking to them

- self-consciousness in front of people and fear of being rejected, humiliated, or embarrassed

- fear of being judged

- worrying for days or weeks before a social event

- avoiding places where there are people

- difficulty making friends and keeping friends

- blushing, sweating, or trembling around other people

- fear of talking to strangers

Situations I fear: _____

_____

_____

☐ *Obsessive-Compulsive Disorder*

The core experience of obsessive-compulsive disorder (OCD) is fear plus compulsive coping behaviors. OCD is a common, chronic anxiety disorder in which a person obsessively thinks about and tries to avoid a specific fear, such as:

- disorganization/forgetting

- germs or contamination

- doing harm (hitting a pedestrian, hurting someone with a knife)

- forbidden or taboo thoughts involving sex, religion, or harm

- aggressive thoughts toward self or others

When a person encounters a situation that triggers the OCD fear (such as driving near a schoolyard, cutting vegetables next to a loved one, touching the latch on a toilet stall, being near someone who might have a disease, making a mistake, and so on), the person will attempt to control the fear with a safety behavior or compulsive ritual. These compulsive behaviors can include:

- excessive cleaning or hand washing

- ordering and arranging things in a particular way

- repeatedly checking on things, such as checking to see if the door is locked or the oven is off, or driving back over the same road to check and see if you hit someone

- compulsive counting

- making ritual gestures (saying or thinking ritual phrases, prayers, or apologies)

- list making to counteract the fear of forgetting

Situations I fear: _____

_____

_____

☐ *Panic Disorder*

People with panic disorder have recurrent, unexpected panic attacks, which are sudden periods of intense fear that may include palpitations, pounding heart, accelerated heart rate, sweating, trembling or shaking, sensations of shortness of breath, the sense of being smothered or choking, or the feeling of impending doom. The core fear is of sensations in your body that are harbingers of panic, and the panic itself.

Panic disorder symptoms include:

- sudden and repeated attacks of intense fear

- feelings of being out of control during a panic attack

- intense worries about when the next attack will happen

- fear or avoidance of places where panic attacks have occurred in the past

Situations I fear: _____

_____

_____

☐ *Specific Phobia*

As the name suggests, a person with specific phobia experiences intense fear in response to a particular object or situation. Fear of blood or needles, fear of enclosed places, and fear of flying are examples of specific phobia. Fear of spiders, fear of snakes, and fear of heights are some more common ones. While many people experience fear of certain situations or things, the key issue with phobia is that the individual feels (1) compelled to avoid it, and (2) the avoidance affects that person's life in a negative way. For example, for a person who lives in New York City, a fear of snakes may not be very concerning. On the other hand, a backpacking guide with a phobia of snakes would need either treatment or a new job.

Situations I fear: _____

_____

_____

☐ *Post-Traumatic Stress Disorder*

Post-traumatic stress disorder (PTSD) can occur after you have been through a traumatic event. A traumatic event is something terrible and scary that you either witness or personally experience, such as:

- combat exposure

- child sexual or physical abuse

- terrorist attack

- sexual or physical assault

- serious accidents, like a car wreck

- natural disasters, like a fire, tornado, hurricane, flood, or earthquake

During a traumatic event, you may fear that your life or others' lives are in danger. You may feel that you have no control over what's happening around you. Most people have some stress-related reactions after a traumatic event, but not everyone experiences PTSD. If your reactions don't go away over time and they disrupt your life, you may have PTSD. Those with PTSD try to avoid situations or people that trigger memories of the traumatic event. They even avoid talking or thinking about the event. If you struggle with PTSD, the way you think about yourself and others may change because of the trauma. You may feel surges of anger, fear, guilt, or shame. You may also experience nightmares or unwanted flashbacks to the event.

Situations I fear: _____

_____

_____

The preceding lists of feared situations will be expanded in the next chapter. But first, the following exercise will help you plan your treatment and how you will use this book. (A downloadable version of this worksheet is available at http://www.newharbinger.com/34749.)

Comprehensive Coping Inventory

The items in this inventory are different ways of dealing with problems. As you complete this inventory, think about difficult or stressful events in your life. Do your best to rate each item in terms of how frequently you use it. There are no right or wrong answers, so choose the most accurate answer for you, not what you think is most acceptable, or what most people would say or do.

Rate each item on a scale of 1 to 5, where 1 means you don't use that strategy at all, and 5 means you use it a great deal.

_____ 1.1   I try to stay away from things that make me anxious or uncomfortable rather than face them.

_____ 1.2   I worry about all the bad things that could happen in the future.

_____ 1.3   When I get upset by a situation, my negative thoughts often don't turn out to be completely true.

_____ 1.4   I don't believe I can cope with situations in which I feel anxious or fearful.

_____ 2.1   I tend to avoid situations, people, places, or things that make me feel anxious or upset.

_____ 2.2   I tend to focus on all the negative outcomes that might result from a decision.

_____ 2.3   I tend to assume things will be worse—more painful and scary—than they turn out to be.

_____ 2.4   I doubt my ability to face situations that trigger anxiety.

_____ 3.1   If I feel anxious and uncomfortable I avoid situations altogether—even though I wish I didn't have to.

_____ 3.2   Whenever there's a problem, I tend to dwell on the worst things that could happen.

_____ 3.3   When the situations are especially upsetting to me, I tend to have a string of thoughts about myself or others that feel true at the time, but often aren't.

_____ 3.4   I don't know how to cope with anxious feelings or situations in which I am fearful.

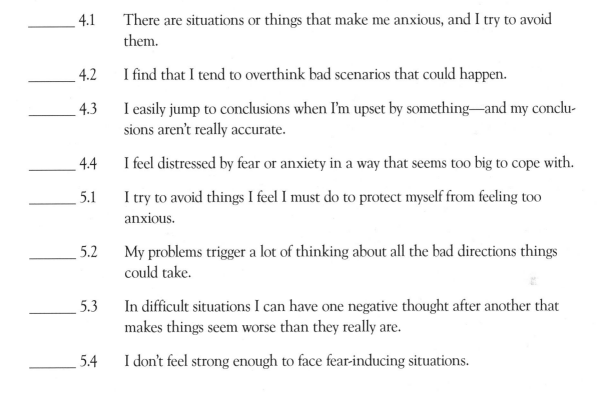

_____ 4.1   There are situations or things that make me anxious, and I try to avoid them.

_____ 4.2   I find that I tend to overthink bad scenarios that could happen.

_____ 4.3   I easily jump to conclusions when I'm upset by something—and my conclusions aren't really accurate.

_____ 4.4   I feel distressed by fear or anxiety in a way that seems too big to cope with.

_____ 5.1   I try to avoid things I feel I must do to protect myself from feeling too anxious.

_____ 5.2   My problems trigger a lot of thinking about all the bad directions things could take.

_____ 5.3   In difficult situations I can have one negative thought after another that makes things seem worse than they really are.

_____ 5.4   I don't feel strong enough to face fear-inducing situations.

You might feel overwhelmed by the number of items that were relevant for you. The good news is that you are bringing awareness to the coping behaviors that are reinforcing your anxiety. This is where the change starts to happen. Let's look at what's significant for you.

1.1, 2.1, 3.1, 4.1, and 5.1 are statements that apply to _avoidance_ of the things that make you feel anxious. These can be people, places, situations, things, or internal sensations that you tend to avoid.

1.2, 2.2, 3.2, 4.2, and 5.2 are statements that apply to _worry/rumination_, extended worrying about future dangers or threats and making negative predictions about the future that get in the way of creating solutions to problems.

1.3, 2.3, 3.3, 4.3, and 5.3 are statements that apply to _cognitive misappraisal_, evaluating a situation, object, sensation, or person as dangerous when it isn't.

1.4, 2.4, 3.4, 4.4, and 5.4 are statements that apply to _distress intolerance_, the belief that you can't stand certain experiences and the emotions they trigger.

Your Treatment Program

Avoidance. If you scored 15 or higher on the inventory items concerning avoidance, you are in good company. You are in exactly the right spot and can confidently go on reading into the next chapter. Avoidance is the number one cause and maintainer of chronic anxiety. Most people who take this inventory score high on avoidance, and nearly half of this book is devoted to ways of solving the avoidance problem.

The number one solution to avoidance, proven in controlled study after controlled study, is *exposure*. Put simply, exposure is solving your anxiety problem by successfully experiencing whatever you are afraid of. The next six chapters of this book take you step by step through the process of exposure. It is a challenging but powerful and comprehensive treatment. Even if you scored relatively low in this section of the inventory, you should work diligently through the next four chapters. Mastering exposure is the key to long-term anxiety treatment.

Worry/rumination. If you scored 15 or higher on the inventory items devoted to rumination, you should supplement the next four chapters by also working through chapter 8, "Reducing Worry with Defusion."

Cognitive misappraisal. If you scored 15 or higher on the items concerning cognitive misappraisal, you can supplement the next four chapters by including the material in chapter 7, "You Can Face Fear," and chapter 9, "Correcting Your Anxiety Lens."

Distress intolerance. If you scored 15 or higher on these items in the inventory, supplement the next four chapters by working on the exercises in chapter 10, "Distress Tolerance Skills."

Finally, don't leave this book without consulting the final chapter 11, "Relapse Prevention," because in the long term you will need a strategy to quickly reapply your anxiety solution skills when you start to feel anxious in the future.

To summarize how to use this book, make sure you do all the work in the next four chapters and chapter 11. Depending on your particular scores on this inventory, you might also benefit from chapters 7 through 10.

Time to Begin

Anxiety takes much of the joy out of life. Every time the alarm bell goes off, you end up feeling endangered and beset with catastrophic possibilities. Your body reacts by preparing for battle or for flight, and demands that you do something to get safe. You feel aroused and over-whelmed, and all you can think about is how to escape the threat.

You must wonder: Can anything help? Could a book like this show the way to relief? The answer is yes. Anxiety isn't a mystery. It isn't a black box that we can't peer into and figure out. Chronic anxiety is caused and maintained by the four factors listed above. The treatment program outlined here will help you target the four factors that turn fear and anxiety from a momentary experience into a disorder.

Help is on the way. Let's get started.

CHAPTER 3

Assessment

In this chapter you will expand your list of feared situations and explore your safety behaviors, including your unique pattern of avoidance. By the end of the chapter you will have a detailed inventory of the people, places, things, situations, and experiences you fear and tend to avoid. You will use this inventory in subsequent chapters, so take your time in this chapter and do the exercises thoroughly.

Get started by transferring your feared situations from the previous chapter to the first column of the worksheet on the following page. (A downloadable version of this worksheet is available at http://www.newharbinger.com/34749.) List all the situations you can think of, including experiences, people, places, things, and even internal experiences such as worrisome thoughts and panicky sensations—everything you fear.

In the second column, rate your SUDS (Subjective Units of Distress) from 0 to 100, where 0 would be *no anxiety* and 100 would be *maximum anxiety possible*.

Leave the third column blank for now.

Exposure Inventory Worksheet

Feared situation	SUDS 0–100	Safety behaviors

Eileen loved horseback riding, but after a fall from her horse she became fearful about riding. Here is her list of feared situations and SUDS ratings.

Eileen's Exposure Inventory Worksheet

Feared situation	SUDS 0–100	Safety behaviors
Cantering in small corral	60	
Riding Meadow Loop Trail	75	
Visiting horse in stable	30	
Remembering/thinking about the fall	50	
Talking about the fall	45	
Galloping	85	
Riding High Ridge Trail	90	
Walking horse in corral	35	

Eileen's feared situations were all related to a particular trauma, the fall from her horse. Depending on the type of anxiety you experience, your list of feared situations might be much more varied.

Safety Behaviors

The next column you will complete on your inventory will be the typical *safety behaviors* you use in response to your feared situations.

What are safety behaviors? We're all hardwired to protect ourselves from dangerous situations. When we experience threat, we'll act quickly and go to great lengths to feel safe. If you were in an unlit parking garage and you heard footsteps behind you, it's likely that you'd move fast to get to the safety of your car. In addition to seeking safety in response to a physically threatening situation, you'll find yourself seeking safety to alleviate the anxiety you experience when you worry about something. Safety behaviors are chosen actions that are carried out to protect you from the emotion of fear, and the catastrophes you worry about.

Safety behaviors are compelling because they provide immediate benefits. They reduce the *feeling* of danger in the short term. For example, if you have OCD, an invitation to dine out may trigger worries about being exposed to germs from the seats and the crowd, the bacteria in the food that's served, and the germs in the public restrooms. If you decline the invitation, thereby avoiding the restaurant and all of the perceived threats that come with it, you'll feel better immediately. If you decide to go, you might take precautions (safety behaviors)—bring antibacterial wipes, wear gloves for the bathroom door, and eat only salad. With these safety behaviors you're alleviating anxiety about contamination, but creating a far greater difficulty. Your fear of germs will continue and perhaps worsen because you haven't done anything to directly decrease the fear itself.

There are two types of safety behaviors: avoidant and approach. With avoidant safety behaviors, you are avoiding, delaying, or escaping the fear. This coping behavior is very appealing because you get an immediate decrease in your level of anxiety. With approach safety behaviors, you engage in the anxiety-provoking situation, but you use strategies that will prevent or minimize your feared outcomes. Both types of safety behaviors make you feel better in the short term. So what's the problem with them?

The problem with using safety behaviors is that you never learn anything. You never learn whether your feared situation or experience will really cause you harm. You never learn to tolerate uncertainty. And you never learn to trust your judgment. So the next time the same threat appears, you suffer the same anxiety, push it away with the same safety behavior, and so on indefinitely. You live in a recursive loop where anxiety tends to become more frequent and intense, not less. The following sequence shows how safety behaviors maintain and often worsen anxiety:

Specific threat creates uncertainty about safety

Worry (thinking about catastrophic things that could happen,
in hopes of reducing uncertainty)

Anxiety/fear increases the longer you worry

Safety behaviors help you avoid or reduce the threat

Anxiety temporarily reduces

No learning takes place—you don't learn to tolerate uncertainty or
learn that the threat won't hurt you

Specific threat reappears

Sequence repeats

Here are some common safety behaviors to consider as you fill in your list:

Avoidance. This is the biggie, the single most important safety behavior, the main engine that powers anxiety. When you avoid what you fear, you reduce your anxiety by taking yourself away from a situation that seems uncertain and threatening. You may avoid situations that involve meeting new people. You might avoid getting your annual checkup because you don't know what the doctor is going to tell you. You might avoid tasks or challenges that bring up fear of failure or danger. At the end of this chapter you will focus in more detail on your unique patterns of avoidance.

Excessive reassurance seeking. If this is one of your safety behaviors, you seek reassurance from others when you are making a decision. This might include making a big decision, like the purchase of a car, or a smaller decision, like what to have for dinner. While it's normal to ask others for their opinions, with this safety behavior the reassurance seeking is *excessive*—as in asking multiple times in order to counteract the anxiety that your worry generates.

Distraction. When facing a feared experience, you might behave in ways that are meant to distract you. This could include daydreaming, compulsive TV watching or Internet use, counting, tapping, planning, and so on. Another form of distraction is looking away from the object or situation that you fear.

Procrastination. Procrastination is a safety behavior that falls under the broader category of avoidance. With procrastination you're putting off a feared experience as a way to delay worrying about something or to minimize your sense of threat or risk.

Checking and double-checking. This safety behavior might manifest as double-checking that you turned off the stove before you leave your home, or checking on loved ones several times a day to make sure they are safe. This is your attempt to feel less anxious when faced with uncertainty.

Overpreparation. The activities related to this safety behavior are designed to increase your certainty about situations that are ambiguous or unpredictable. Maybe you've heard the expression, "I'm anxious about anything I can't Google." You will seek out as much information and prepare yourself as much as possible to decrease the level of uncertainty when you face an anxiety-provoking challenge.

Perfectionism. The goal of this safety behavior is to eliminate uncertainty and mistakes by doing everything flawlessly. This means not delegating tasks to others so you can make sure they get done the way that you want. It can also mean overworking to avoid the possibility of errors.

Rituals. When facing a feared situation, you may engage in rituals as a safety behavior. As soon as you think of something bad happening to people you love, you might say a prayer to keep them safe, or you may arrange objects in a specific way. You may carry specific objects with you as a way to keep yourself safe (such as a lucky charm, a keepsake, or a photo).

List making. Creating lists to avoid forgetting and uncertainty is a common safety behavior.

Drugs/alcohol/anxiety medications. Using drugs or alcohol to try to mute anxiety is a safety behavior, as is carrying anxiety medication (just in case).

Take your time filling in column 2. Identify the safety behaviors you use when encountering each of your feared situations and experiences. What exactly do you do to cope with the anxiety these experiences trigger? How do you get away from or diminish your fear?

Here is Eileen's inventory with her safety behaviors added:

Feared situation	SUDS 0–100	Safety behaviors
Cantering in small corral	60	Holding saddle horn the whole time
Riding Meadow Loop Trail	75	Procrastinating/avoiding riding, or riding with instructor
Visiting horse in stable	30	Procrastinating, or constantly saying "Good boy!"
Remembering/thinking about the fall	50	Distracting myself with my iPhone
Talking about the fall	45	Distracting by changing subject
Galloping	85	Avoiding, thinking I can ride later with instructor
Riding High Ridge Trail	90	Avoiding, thinking I can ride later with instructor
Walking horse in corral	35	Constant reassurance seeking with riding instructor

Focusing on Avoidance

There are three kinds of avoidant safety behaviors that people use in an attempt to control anxiety: situational, cognitive, and sensation or interoceptive avoidance. As you read the descriptions below, put a check mark next to the type(s) of avoidance you've used. It's not unusual for people to use all three, so don't be discouraged if that's the case. This program will help you no matter what forms of avoidance you use.

☐ **Situational avoidance.** This is the most common type of avoidance. You stay away from activities, places, people, and things that tend to trigger your anxiety. For example, when Scott was a child, a dog bit his hand when he tried to pet it. Scott remained fearful of dogs. As an adult, he would not attend any functions at the homes of friends who owned a dog, and he avoided parks and other outdoor venues that allowed dogs. In the short term, Scott was able to avoid the feelings that got triggered when he was near a dog, but in the long term he missed out on experiences with friends and loved ones.

☐ **Cognitive avoidance.** This type of avoidance is specific to what takes place in your mind. You expend great effort to get rid of distressing thoughts or disturbing memories by making conscious attempts to suppress them. This might involve replacing them with more pleasant or distracting content such as fantasies, daydreams, mantras, prayers, or other thought rituals. Or you might try suppressing distressing thoughts with drugs, alcohol, high-risk behaviors, binge eating, self-harm, and so on. For example, Ellen struggled to push away memories of molestation by a neighbor when she was nine. When the memories came up, she drank, picked fights with her boyfriend, binged on reality TV and ice cream, and made covert plans to move out of state. She also avoided sexual experiences that reminded her of the molestation. Despite her efforts at suppression, memories of the trauma still came up, alongside feelings of being somehow bad and wrong. Not only did Ellen's cognitive avoidance not work to avoid anxiety, but it also resulted in a drinking problem, loss of her relationship, social withdrawal, and depression—a feeling that she was failing at life.

☐ **Sensation/interoceptive avoidance.** With sensation or interoceptive avoidance, your efforts are focused on avoiding internal sensations such as feeling hot, feeling tired, labored breathing, or rapid heartbeat. You may even avoid pleasant sensations, such as sexual excitement or excitement about an event, because they feel similar to anxiety sensations. For example, Juan had a panic attack on a gridlocked freeway where there had been a major accident. During the panic he felt dizzy, hot, and shaky, had palpitations, and felt "totally out of it." Since that time, he fears and vigilantly watches for any of these sensations. He tries desperately to stop or block them, avoiding places where they might occur. As a consequence, Juan is now avoiding all exercise so he won't get heart palpitations or overheated or too excited. He doesn't watch sports, go to concerts, hike, or go on outings with friends. What's worse, if Juan even anticipates the possibility of panic, he begins to feel dizzy and "out of it"—which often triggers a full-blown attack.

After focusing on the types of avoidance, you might find that you can break some items on your inventory down into more components. For example, a fear of crowded places might include the following items:

- crowded restaurants

- movie theaters

- concerts/nightclubs

- shopping malls

- supermarket checkout lines

Or a fear of germs might include:

- bathroom doorknobs

- public doorknobs

- touching toilet flush lever

- touching money

- going to doctors' offices

- touching stair railings

Go back to your inventory and expand any of the feared situations or safety behaviors that could use more detail.

When Eileen considered the three types of avoidance, she realized that she used cognitive avoidance any time she even thought about riding on the higher trails. And she drilled down into her real fears to realize that what caused her the most distress was the possibility of experiencing again the physical sensations of panic that she felt when her horse threw her on a steep trail. So she added items 9 and 10 to her inventory:

Eileen's Exposure Inventory Worksheet

Feared situation	SUDS 0–100	Safety behaviors
Cantering in small corral	60	Holding saddle horn the whole time
Riding Meadow Loop Trail	75	Procrastinating/avoiding riding, or riding with instructor
Visiting horse in stable	30	Procrastinating, or constantly saying "Good boy!"
Remembering/thinking about the fall	50	Distracting myself with my iPhone
Talking about the fall	45	Distracting by changing subject
Galloping	85	Avoiding, thinking I can ride later with instructor
Riding High Ridge Trail	90	Avoiding, thinking I can ride later with instructor
Walking horse in corral	35	Constant reassurance seeking with riding instructor
Thinking about riding difficult trails	*45*	*Distracting with iPhone*
Panicky physical sensation of not being in control when horse thrusts up on steep trails	*100*	*Avoiding, thinking I can ride later with instructor*

In the next chapter you will work on motivation, exploring why it is worth it to you to use exposure and the other techniques in this book to solve your anxiety problems.

CHAPTER 4

Motivation

It is not easy to stop your safety behaviors and expose yourself to experiences you would rather avoid. You're going to need the motivation that this chapter will provide. First you will examine the negative consequences of avoidance and other safety behaviors. Then you will review your life values, especially the activities and relationships you've been missing out on because of your anxiety. Finally, you will assess your willingness to go forward with your treatment plan.

Costs of Avoidance

As you become more familiar with your avoidance and other safety behaviors, you may also be thinking about the ways in which you are missing out on important aspects of your life. The more you avoid, the more your life is limited. Avoidance affects you emotionally, creating depression when you stop doing things you enjoy or find nurturing. When you continually disappoint or upset your family and friends, your relationships suffer and you feel shame and guilt. Safety behaviors are likely creating consequences at work or school as well, blocking you from reaching some of your life goals or preventing you from getting in touch with your life purpose. And, by continuing to engage in safety behaviors, you never learn that there is less to fear than you believe.

The following worksheet will help you identify the costs of avoidance. (This worksheet is available for download at http://www.newharbinger.com/34749.) In each of the following domains, list your avoidance or other safety behaviors and their negative impact on your life. Rate the impact on your life from 1 (very little negative impact) to 5 (large negative impact).

Cost of Avoidance Worksheet

Domain	Avoidance or other safety behaviors	Negative impact on my life	Rating 1–5
Friendships			
Family			
Parenting			
Work/education			
Self-care/health			
Pleasure, recreation, social activities			
Life goals			
Service to others			
Romantic relationships			

Laura used the Cost of Avoidance Worksheet to examine how her fear of being socially judged or rejected was affecting her life. In particular, Laura feared talking to strangers, believing that they might discover something flawed or unacceptable about her. She even worried about friends secretly disliking her. Social situations frequently triggered thoughts like *I'm stupid*, *I'm boring*, or *I'm unattractive*.

Laura's Cost of Avoidance Worksheet

Domain	Avoidance or other safety behaviors	Negative impact on my life	Rating 1–5
Friendships	Won't go to parties or social events with friends.	Loneliness, don't meet anyone, friends upset at me.	4
	Keep checking to see if things are okay between us.	Friends annoyed, seem to withdraw.	3
	Avoid calling and initiating contact.	Friends withdraw, rarely see them.	5
Family			
Parenting			
Work/education	Avoid talking to coworkers.	Feel isolated at work, no real work friends.	4
	Try to do everything perfectly.	Huge stress, constantly afraid of mistakes and disapproval.	4
Self-care/health			
Pleasure, recreation, social activities	Drink at all social events to stop feeling like a failure.	Feel out of it and stupid. Can't have a sensible conversation.	3
	Go online to distract myself at social events.	Feel isolated and alone at social events.	3
	Avoid team sports.	Couldn't play softball.	3
	Avoid fun group activities.	Loneliness	4

Domain	Avoidance or other safety behaviors	Negative impact on my life	Rating 1–5
Life goals	Ritual thoughts like *I'm doing my best* when I feel sad about no relationship and being alone.	Ignore sadness and do nothing about how alone I am.	5
Service to others	Procrastinated joining sustainability advocacy group.	Feel like I'm failing to try to make the world better.	5
Romantic relationships	Procrastinated setting up online dating profile.	Not meeting anyone, alone.	5
	Procrastinated joining singles hiking group.	Not enjoying nature, loneliness.	5

As a result of this exercise, Laura noticed that her safety behaviors were directly linked to her loneliness, isolation at work, and feelings of disconnection from friends. Even worse, the sense of hopelessness about ever having a romantic relationship seemed to be a direct outcome of her safety behaviors.

Values

Now instead of focusing on the negative aspects of your anxiety, think about the positive things you would like to do if anxiety weren't paralyzing you. What activities and abilities have you lost? What plans can you no longer make? What goals have you given up? What sources of joy or fulfillment seem closed to you now? In short, what do you care about? What are your life values?

The following worksheet will help clarify some of the valued activities your anxiety has curtailed. (A downloadable version of this worksheet is available at http://www.newharbinger.com/34749.) In the left-hand column, list your specific fears. In the middle column, identify each valued activity the fear blocks. Note that each fear could prevent multiple activities in multiple settings (work, recreation, family activities, social activities, health maintenance, parenting, and so on). In the right-hand column, rate how important each activity is from 1 (slightly valued) to 5 (extremely valued).

Values Worksheet

Fear (Things I avoid)	Blocked valued activities	Values rating 1–5

Naomi, who had a fear of contamination, listed multiple situations she avoided on her Values Worksheet. She was surprised to see how each of these feared situations blocked activities that she valued.

Naomi's Values Worksheet

Fear (Things I avoid)	Blocked valued activities	Values rating 1–5
Public restrooms	Can't go shopping with friends	3
	Can't go hiking	2
	Can't go to gym	2
	Can't travel	5
	Can't see Mom in NY	5
	Can't go to concerts	5
	Can't work in an office	5
	Can't go on dates	5
Sick people	Can't use public transportation	1
	Can't go to theaters	2
	Can't go to hospital for my knee operation	5
	Can't see doctor	4
Dirt	Can't do pottery or grow orchids	4
	Can't visit my brother in his filthy apartment	4
	Can't get on the floor	1
Herbicides/pesticides	Can't get on grass	3
	Can't go into people's gardens	2
	Can't go to the park	2

As Naomi examined her worksheet, it became clear that her fear of public toilets was preventing many highly valued activities. Her fear of sick people was also blocking a needed knee surgery, and preventing her from taking adequate care of her health. Her fear of dirt was getting in the way of two valued hobbies—pottery and orchid raising—as well as seeing her brother. Fear was costing her a great deal in areas that deeply mattered to her. As a result of this process, she was beginning to recognize the situations where she was most willing to face challenging exposures.

Notice that values help guide your life toward things that matter to you. Because anxiety often makes it difficult to act on key values, anxiety can rob your life of meaning. You may end up avoiding many of the activities and experiences you care most about. This is how anxiety can co-occur with depression: anxiety gets in the way of meaningful activities, and the resulting loss of vitality and engagement causes you to spiral down into depression.

The Importance of Willingness

Unwillingness lies at the root of avoidance. Very understandably, you've been unwilling to feel the anxiety and distress associated with situations that scare you. You've wanted to keep your distance from the *feeling* of danger, from that sensation in your stomach that says harm is imminent.

The process of recovering from anxiety asks you to become *willing*, to allow yourself to feel the emotions and physical sensations connected to the things you fear. We are encouraging you to say "yes" to the hot flush, the electric sensation in your spine, the sudden weakness in your legs, the light-headed feeling, the knot in your stomach. We are asking you to say "yes" to feeling vulnerable, to feeling unsafe, to adrenaline and fear.

Willingness to feel everything associated with a feared situation, no matter how long or how strong, is the road to recovery and freedom. Willingness to accept the butterflies, willingness to accept the thought that you won't survive, willingness to accept a sense of doom—all of this is the path to liberation from anxiety.

As you prepare for your exposures in the next two chapters, whatever the specific situations, whatever length of time you'll spend facing your fear, the question is always willingness. Will you be willing to feel everything there is to feel in this situation, for this length of time? Willingness is the commitment to feel 100 percent of the experience, to stay for the allotted period of exposure, and to allow yourself to face *whatever there is*.

You will need willingness in the work ahead. You will need to say yes to fear—in your body and your mind. And in saying yes you'll be finally set free from the long night of anxiety that has ruled your life.

CHAPTER 5

Preparation

In this chapter you will complete your Exposure Inventory Worksheet: a detailed plan for how to stop safety behaviors and systematically expose yourself to what you've been avoiding. Your inventory builds on all the work you have done to this point: listing your feared situations and experiences, examining your safety behaviors in detail, and putting numerical values on the negative distress you feel and the positive values by which you want to live your life.

Planning

To further refine your inventory you will add a plan to stop safety behaviors, as well as "predicted outcomes," and "percent probability" to each of your feared situations. On the following worksheet, write down one of your feared situations, your associated safety behaviors, the subjective units of distress (SUDS), and the relative value ratings you made in the previous chapters. (This worksheet is available to download at http://www.newharbinger.com/34749.)

Exposure Inventory Worksheet

Feared situation	Safety behaviors	Plan to stop safety behavior and to expose	SUDS 1–100	Value 1–5	Predicted worst-case outcome	Percent probability

In the third column, make a plan for stopping your safety behaviors and exposing yourself to what you have been avoiding. There are two ways to do this: the cold turkey plan and the gradual plan.

Cold Turkey Plan

In this plan, you immediately stop the distraction, reassurance seeking, procrastination, and so on—all the things you have been doing to soften or postpone facing your anxiety. And you immediately *do* the things you have been avoiding doing. You dive right into the cold water of the feared situation.

Remember Eileen, the equestrian who became anxious about riding her horse? She made a cold turkey plan to handle many of her feared situations:

Eileen's Exposure Inventory Worksheet, Cold Turkey Plan

Feared situation	Safety behaviors	Plan to stop safety behavior and to expose	SUDS 1–100	Value 1–5	Predicted worst-case outcome	Percent probability
Cantering	Holding saddle horn	Hold reins, don't touch saddle horn	60	3		
Visiting horse	Procrastinate, say "Good boy!" constantly	Visit twice a week, no "Good boy"	30	3		
Remembering the fall	Distraction	Plan on four 20-minute sessions recalling accident and hospital stay	50	4		
Talking about the fall	Avoiding any mention of it	Get Mom to listen to the whole story—30 minutes	45	4		
Walking horse in corral	Seeking reassurance from instructor	Send instructor out of earshot	35	3		
Thinking about difficult trails	Distracting with iPhone	Think about them for 15 minutes without distraction	45	5		

Gradual Plan

The second way to discontinue safety behaviors is to reduce them more gradually. You can create a hierarchy that goes from full use of the safety behavior, to partial use, and incrementally to no use. The trick is to devise two to five steps that can cushion the shock of a cold-turkey plunge into zero safety behaviors. Plan a gradual lessening of safety behaviors if you sense that your anxiety will be too overwhelming with a cold turkey approach. Of course, there is a downside to gradual plans: they take a lot longer.

Here's how Eileen made gradual plans for riding the Meadow Loop Trail and overcoming panic sensations on steep trails:

Eileen's Exposure Inventory Worksheet, Gradual Plan

Feared situation	Safety behaviors	Plan to stop safety behavior and to expose	SUDS 1–100	Value 1–5	Predicted worst-case outcome	Percent probability
Riding Meadow Loop Trail	Procrastinating, avoiding, or riding only with instructor	Ride with instructor leading the way Ride with instructor behind me Ride alone with instructor on speed dial Ride alone	75	4		
Panicky feeling when horse thrusts up on steep trails	Avoiding, postponing, saying maybe I'll ride with instructor	Stand at foot of grade and watch instructor ride it Ride the grade with instructor watching Ride the grade with instructor on speed dial Ride alone	100	5		

Here are some other ways to gradually eliminate other typical safety behaviors:

- For *overpreparation*, cutting preparation time in increments until it reaches an appropriate level

- Waiting longer and longer periods to *seek reassurance*

- Cutting time spent in *distraction*, or changing the types of distraction

- Limiting *procrastination* time by setting a deadline or completing the exposure in increments

- For *avoidance*, doing part but not all of an exposure, then working up to the full exposure

- *Checking* less and less frequently

- For *perfectionism*, making deliberate mistakes—first one, then two, then three

- Reducing time spent doing a *ritual* until it reaches nothing; cutting the number of words in a ritual prayer or coping thought; using the ritual half the time, then a quarter of the time, and so on

- For *list making*, creating shorter lists and setting a limit for how much time you will spend on lists.

- Reducing the quantity, frequency, and/or potency of *drug and alcohol* consumption.

Predicting Worst-Case Outcomes

The false alarms that have plagued you and driven your struggle with anxiety can't be overcome with reasoning. You can't argue away your fears. You've no doubt tried—or others have—and the alarm reactions just keep happening. When it comes to anxiety, and the belief that certain things or situations are dangerous, you can't think your way out of it. Only real, disconfirming experiences can change deeply held beliefs. This is true for all of us—we literally have to be *shown* that our beliefs about danger aren't true before they can change. We have to experience the thing we've feared and have something other than what we expected happen.

The mismatch between the harmful thing you expect and actual outcomes is critical to new learning. And the more your expectation is contradicted by direct experience, the more powerfully your old beliefs about danger will be disconfirmed. Overcoming false alarms, and all the avoidance they generate, involves predicting that a particular aversive outcome will occur (from an exposure) and then carefully comparing actual outcomes to the prediction.

In the sixth column of your Exposure Inventory Worksheet, for each of your plans, you need to make a prediction: what are you most afraid will happen if you follow your plan and stop your safety behavior? This prediction should be expressed as *observable* behavior—yours or others'—as opposed to your feelings and internal experiences. For example, individuals who fear elevators might predict that the doors will close and they will be stuck between floors. Or that the cable will break and the elevator will start to drop. Or that they will have a heart attack while riding the elevator. Notice that the prediction doesn't include how the individual will feel, but rather focuses on a worst-case scenario of what is expected to happen.

While there is no point predicting that you'll feel anxiety—because you will—you can predict your own behavioral responses. Returning to the elevator example, a behavioral prediction might look like this: "I'll be so overwhelmed, I'll push the button for the next floor, get off, take the stairs down, and go home." You can also predict other people's behavior in response to your tests. For example, a socially anxious woman, who is afraid of asking questions, predicted the following: "When I ask department store clerks about the quality and durability of a particular item, they'll get a contemptuous look, say (in so many words) my question is ridiculous, and walk away from me." Notice the prediction doesn't center on how the clerk feels or what the clerk thinks. There's no way to observe and know that. The prediction is based entirely on outcomes you can see—they either happen or they don't.

Go back and write in your worst fears and exactly what will happen if they come true.

Percent Probability

The next step in the prediction process is to assess how likely it is that the feared outcome will take place. For example, you might assess that there is "an 80 percent chance that standing next to a dog will result in getting bit." Or that there is "a 70 percent chance I'll cut myself or someone else if I use a chopping knife." Or that there is "a 90 percent chance I'll be so scared I'll have to get off the subway before reaching my stop." For each of your worst-case outcomes, note the percent probability in the last column.

Notice that the percent probability isn't based on actual odds, but on what your fear tells you. For example, you may know rationally that millions of people use knives every day without mishap. But your assessment of the probability of injury should be based on your *feeling* of danger and your subjective belief about likely outcomes if *you* use a knife.

Completing Your List of Feared Situations

Continue listing all your feared situations on your inventory, with safety behaviors, plans, and so on, until all columns are filled in. Take your time and do a thorough job. Remember, the basic solution to anxiety is simple: avoid what you usually do, and do what you usually avoid. But the implementation can be complex, layered, subtle, and time-consuming.

Examples

To help you figure out how to make better exposure plans and outcome predictions, the rest of this chapter consists of detailed examples of other people's inventories. There is at least one example for each of the six anxiety disorders. Some disorders have more than one example, to show the widest possible range of options in filling out an exposure inventory.

Look through all of the examples, even if you don't suffer from the particular type of anxiety exemplified. You will learn different ways to structure your inventory to create a list of doable exposure experiences. Notice how others:

- combine two mildly feared situations to make one more scary situation

- break a very scary situation down into several less scary situations

- make a plan gradual by altering the distance in time or space to a feared object

- include visualizations of past experiences or imagined scenes, which tends to increase expectations that the predicted worst-case outcomes will happen

- keep predicted outcomes behavioral and observable, not feeling-based

- set higher percent probabilities based on subjective fear, not actuarial data

Generalized Anxiety Disorder (GAD)— Stephan's Rumination

Stephan struggled with a harsh "worry voice" that plagued him with frequent rumination about his health, his job, money, and crime. Notice that his feared situations all have the excessive worry component so typical of generalized anxiety disorder. Note that Stephan highly valued learning to face medical fears and getting free of constant worry about his symptoms.

Stephan's Exposure Inventory Worksheet

Feared situation	Safety behaviors	Plan to stop safety behavior and to expose	SUDS 1–100	Value 1–5	Predicted worst-case outcome	Percent probability
Thinking doctor is wrong and stomach pain is not just gas	Lots of online medical research	Just stop cold turkey	85	5	Undetected stomach cancer will make me keep getting sicker.	65%
Worrying I'll lose everything when stock market goes down	Constantly check Dow and S&P, call broker for reassurance	Check twice today, once tomorrow, skip a day, once more, then stop cold. Call broker only once a quarter.	75	4	Market will tank soon and I'll be wiped out, homeless.	50%
Assuming if I buy a new Buick it will be a lemon	Rechecking Consumer Reports, procrastinating, frequent test drives, reassurance seeking with friends	Drive each of five models once, then decide	60	2	I'll pay high end for a car and just keep pouring money down a bottomless pit.	70%

Feared situation	Safety behaviors	Plan to stop safety behavior and to expose	SUDS 1–100	Value 1–5	Predicted worst-case outcome	Percent probability
Thinking about recent mass shooting as I'm going to a concert—I'll be killed	Seeking reassurance from friends, checking news stories about terrorist activities	No more reassurance conversations, stay off news sites	65	3	Concert will be targeted by a deranged shooter and I'll get shot, or at least trampled in the stampede.	60%
Afraid of getting fired when boss asks for a meeting	Ask colleagues for reassurance	Stop talking to colleagues about boss and performance reviews	90	4	I'll lose my job, then my house, then my wife and kids.	90%
Fearing heart attack when heart rate goes up at gym	Constantly taking pulse, online medical research at home	Stop cold turkey	70	5	I'll collapse on the treadmill with a heart attack.	70%

Social Anxiety—Antonio's Fear of Socializing

Antonio is lonely. His last girlfriend was six years ago in college, someone who asked *him* out. His fear of being judged or rejected has kept him from:

- talking to female coworkers

- talking to fellow commuters

- going to parties or work gatherings

- going to Meetup groups

- putting up a profile for online dating

- asking someone on a date

- going to political meetings or events (Antonio is interested in conservation, ecology, and the Green Movement)

Antonio's exposure inventory for social anxiety is typical in that it involves two types of exposure:

1. **Situations** that will induce him to speak with others, particularly people to whom he's attracted.

2. **Visualizations** of worst-case scenarios in which his attempts at conversation are met with scorn and rejection.

Notice that Antonio highly values any exposures involving contact with Irene, someone he likes at work.

Antonio's Exposure Inventory Worksheet

Feared situation	Safety behaviors	Plan to stop safety behavior and to expose	SUDS 1–100	Value 1–5	Predicted worst-case outcome	Percent probability
Talking to others	Avoid it, keep quiet, don't go to parties and other events	Say "hello" to Irene at her desk	50	5	She'll shrug, avoid eye contact, and look away	60
		Put up online dating profile	60	3	Too scary, won't finish it and hit "submit"	80
		Go to "Save the Earth" Meetup group	65	4	No one will talk to me	70
		Start a conversation with Irene about her vacation	70	5	She'll look away and ignore me	70
		Go to singles bar—30 min.	70	2	No one will talk to me	85
		Go to after-hours office party—30 min.	75	2	I won't talk to anyone, they won't talk to me	80
		Respond via e-mail to 5 interesting profiles	75	3	No one will respond to me	90

Feared situation	Safety behaviors	Plan to stop safety behavior and to expose	SUDS 1–100	Value 1–5	Predicted worst-case outcome	Percent probability
Talking to others	Avoid it, keep quiet, don't go to parties and other events	Go to party at my sister's house	80	2	I won't say a word to anyone, no one will talk to me	75
		Make a small (hopefully funny) remark to someone on train	80	2	They'll look disgusted, refuse to speak to me	80
		Go on Sierra Club Singles hike and talk to 2 people	90	3	They'll look offended, move away from me	95
Being rejected	Avoid	Visualize talking to woman on train who looks disgusted and moves away	55	1	Have to stop, too painful	60
Combos	Avoid	Visualize being scorned + conversation with Irene	70	1	She'll say she's busy and look away	95
		Visualize being scorned + go to singles bar—no alcohol	95	3	People will avoid me, they'll move away when I speak to them	100

By now you should have a pretty long Exposure Inventory Worksheet, probably rewritten a few times as you revise your plans for stopping safety behaviors and exposing yourself to your feared situations. In the next chapter you will finally get a chance to put your inventory to use, and start solving your anxiety problems with positive actions.

Obsessive-Compulsive Disorder (OCD)— Mary's Fear of Doing Harm

Mary feared harming her two-year-old daughter or her husband with a sharp implement such as a knife, serving fork, scissors, or needle. She reached the point where she was afraid to cook or sew, particularly if her daughter or husband were anywhere near. Her exposure inventory included holding and then using sharp implements, as well as visualizing accidentally cutting her daughter with a knife. Notice that items involving shared activities with her daughter are highly valued.

Mary's Exposure Inventory Worksheet

Feared situation	Safety behaviors	Plan to stop safety behavior and to expose	SUDS 1–100	Value 1–5	Predicted worst-case outcome	Percent probability
Picking up paring knife or carving knife, especially near husband or daughter	Avoid it, wait until they're gone	Holding carving knife—1 min.	60	2	Drop knife or cut myself	70
		Holding carving knife—3 min.	70	2	Drop knife or cut myself	80
		Holding paring knife—1 min., husband across kitchen	70	2	Cut husband	60
		Holding paring knife—3 min., daughter across kitchen	80	2	Cut daughter	75
		Holding carving knife and fork, daughter across kitchen	80	2	Cut or stab daughter	75
		Holding carving knife and fork, daughter near cutting board	90	2	Cut or stab daughter	85
Chopping	Avoid it, buy precut veggies	Chopping 5 carrots, salad, daughter across kitchen	85	3	Cut daughter	80

Feared situation	Safety behaviors	Plan to stop safety behavior and to expose	SUDS 1–100	Value 1–5	Predicted worst-case outcome	Percent probability
Chopping	Avoid it, buy precut veggies	Chopping 10 apples for pie, daughter near cutting board	95	4	Cut daughter	95
Sewing with needles, cutting cloth with scissors	Only do it alone or not at all	Cutting cloth, living room, daughter across room	70	4	Cut daughter	70
		Cutting cloth, living room, daughter near me	85	5	Cut daughter	90
		Hand sewing her costume, daughter across room	65	4	Poke daughter with needle	70
		Hand sewing her costume, daughter near me	75	4	Poke daughter with needle	80
Thinking about cutting daughter	Distraction with TV, Internet,	Visualize daughter cut by knife	70	1	I'll have to stop visualizing, distract myself	80
Combos	Avoid	Visualize daughter cut and sewing with her near	95	5	Poke daughter with needle	90
		Visualize daughter cut and chopping with her near	100	3	Cut daughter	100

55

Obsessive-Compulsive Disorder (OCD)— Annalea's Fear of Contamination

Annalea had struggled with a fear of germs since her college roommate contracted mono-nucleosis and had to drop out of school. She became increasingly vigilant in looking out for any possibility of contamination. She avoided touching doorknobs, railings, toilets, floors, chair seats, paper money, and other people—particularly their hands. When Annalea touched something she believed to be contaminated, she suffered extreme anxiety until she washed or showered. Washing rituals could last up to several hours, and on bad days Annalea spent much of her time compulsively "de-germing" herself. She strongly valued her relationships, as you'll see in exposure items involving family and friends.

Annalea's Exposure Inventory Worksheet

Feared situation	Safety behaviors	Plan to stop safety behavior and to expose	SUDS 1–100	Value 1–5	Predicted worst-case outcome	Percent probability
Touching doorknobs	Avoiding, washing	Touching inside doorknob for 10 seconds, washing only 3 min. after toilet and before meals, no other washing	40	1	Sick by bedtime	60
		Touching outside doorknob for 10 sec., washing only 2 min. after toilet, before meals, no other washing	60	3	Sick by bedtime	80
Being near sick people	Avoiding, washing	Visualize seeing roommate in hospital	40	4	Can't stand it, have to stop	60
Touching floor	Avoiding, washing	Both hands on living room floor for 30 sec., washing 2 min. only after toilet, before meals	65	2	Sick by bedtime	70
Touching other people	Avoidance	Shaking hands with friends at a political meeting, washing 1 min. after toilet, before meals	80	4	Sick by bedtime	95

THE CBT ANXIETY SOLUTION WORKBOOK

Feared situation	Safety behaviors	Plan to stop safety behavior and to expose	SUDS 1–100	Value 1–5	Predicted worst-case outcome	Percent probability
Touching other people	Avoidance	Hugging mother, 1 min., washing as above	45	5	Sick by bedtime	60
		Taking mother's arm to help her walk, washing as above	60	5	Sick by bedtime	70
Touching money	Avoiding, washing	Counting money in wallet, washing as above	70	3	Sick by bedtime	75
		Counting money from ATM, washing as above	80	3	Sick by bedtime	85
Touching toilet	Avoiding, washing	Lower toilet seat with my hand, washing as above	100	2	Sick by bedtime	100
Touching chairs and railings	Avoiding, washing	Hands on armchair, washing only 30 sec.	70	2	Sick by bedtime	60
		Hands on my mother's armchair, washing 30 sec.	80	3	Sick by bedtime	65
		Hands on park bench seat, washing 30 sec.	75	1	Sick by bedtime	80
		Hands on store stair railing, washing 30 sec.	70	2	Sick by bedtime	85

Feared situation	Safety behaviors	Plan to stop safety behavior and to expose	SUDS 1–100	Value 1–5	Predicted worst-case outcome	Percent probability
Touching floor	Avoiding, washing	Both hands on bathroom floor—30 sec., washing 30 sec.	100	3	Sick by bedtime	95
Near sick people, touching sick people	Avoiding, washing	Visualize roommate in hospital + shaking hands with friends, washing 30 sec.	90	4	Sick by bedtime	100
		Visualize roommate in hospital + counting money from ATM, washing 30 sec.	85	3	Sick by bedtime	90
Touching doorknobs and money	Avoiding, washing	Hand on store doorknob + count money, washing 30 sec.	95	3	Sick by bedtime	95

This example showed Annalea's inventory for exposing herself to her contamination fears and discontinuing her safety behavior of prolonged hand washing. While not fully shown in her inventory, she also systematically reduced the time she spent showering. In the end, she tapered down to showering once a day for ten minutes and washing her hands for only thirty seconds before each meal and after using the bathroom.

Obsessive-Compulsive Disorder (OCD) —Morgan's Forbidden Thoughts

Morgan, the son of missionaries, lost his girlfriend in a car accident when she was only thirty-one. At the funeral he had the sudden thought, *I hate God.* The thought was so disturbing and unacceptable that he tried to banish it from his mind. But the more he tried to avoid the thought, the more frequently it appeared. As a way of undoing or neutralizing the thought, he whispered, "Sorry, sorry, sorry," each time it occurred.

Morgan's inventory first worked on stopping his ritual "Sorry, sorry, sorry" safety behavior, then concentrated on tolerating the *I hate God* phrase as a thought alone, as a thought in certain situations, when said out loud, and when written down.

Morgan's Exposure Inventory Worksheet

Feared situation	Safety behaviors	Plan to stop safety behavior and to expose	SUDS 1–100	Value 1–5	Predicted worst-case outcome	Percent probability
Thinking my *I hate God* thought	Ritual: whispering "Sorry, sorry, sorry." Trying to avoid the thought	Shorten to two sorries for a day, then one sorry for the next day, then no sorries thereafter	80	3	I won't be able to stop. If I do stop, God will physically strike me down.	75
		Think my thought once alone	55	1	Physically struck down	60
		Think it 10 times	70	1	Physically struck down	65
		Think it 50 times	85	1	Physically struck down	70
		Think it while talking to clients	70	3	They'll know, and will cancel their contract	90
		Think it while with parents	90	3	They'll read my mind	60
		Think it in church	100	1	Physically struck down	100

Feared situation	Safety behaviors	Plan to stop safety behavior and to expose	SUDS 1–100	Value 1–5	Predicted worst-case outcome	Percent probability
Writing down the thought	"Sorry, sorry."	Write it once	65	3	Physically struck down	60
		Look at it and read it for 5 minutes	90	3	Physically struck down	60
		Write it 10 times	70	3	Physically struck down	70
		Write it 50 times	90	3	Physically struck down	80
		Write it on big sheet of sketch paper	80	2	Physically struck down	85
Saying the thought out loud	"Sorry, sorry."	Say it once while alone in the car	70	2	Physically struck down	80
		Tell my friend Alex about my thought	95	3	He'll reject me	95

Panic Disorder—Sergio's Fear of Travel

Sergio had his first panic attack in a hotel, following a turbulent and stressful plane flight. The physical symptoms included feeling dizzy/light-headed and flushed, rapid heart rate, a sense that he couldn't get enough air, and weakness in his legs. Subsequent panic attacks were at first rare, occurring only when he traveled far from home. As time went by, they began to happen on public transportation, in crowded places, on long drives, and when caught in traffic, always preceded by one or more of his physical symptoms. If you look at the values column in Sergio's inventory below, you'll see that his fear of panic attacks kept him from enjoying activities he valued very highly, such as movies, eating out, and spending time with friends.

Note that Sergio's inventory contains situational, interoceptive, and imagery-based exposures. His panic disorder was typical in that what he dreaded was not so much certain situations, but rather the *interoceptive physical sensations* of panic that he might feel in those situations. For exposure to work in treating panic disorder, it helps to design safe, controllable experiences that will reproduce similar physical sensations. Sergio recreated the interoceptive experiences as follows:

Panic symptom	Interoceptive equivalent
Rapid heart rate	Running in place
Flushed/hot feeling	Running in place with heavy coat
Dizziness/light-headedness	Very rapid breathing
Difficulty breathing	Breathing through a straw
Leg weakness	Holding a "half squat" until legs feel weak/shaky

Sergio's Exposure Inventory Worksheet

Feared situation	Safety behaviors	Plan to stop safety behavior and to expose	SUDS 1–100	Value 1–5	Predicted worst-case outcome	Percent probability
Driving more than a few miles	Avoidance: stay home, get rides	Drive to San Rafael—30 min.	45	2	Panic, have to stop	60
		Drive to Napa—60 min.	55	2	Panic, have to stop	70
		Drive to Clear Lake—2 hrs.	70	5	Panic, have to stop	75
Thinking about my first panic	Distraction, drinking, Internet	Visualize 1st panic—2 min., then 5 min., no distraction or numbing	45	1	Can't stand it, have to stop	60
Taking public transportation	Avoidance	BART train to Oakland	50	1	Panic, have to get off	60
		BART train to S.F.	70	3	Panic, have to get off	60
		Bus to Sacramento	80	4	Panic, have to get off	75
		Bus to Reno	90	5	Panic, have to get off	95

Feared situation	Safety behaviors	Plan to stop safety behavior and to expose	SUDS 1–100	Value 1–5	Predicted worst-case outcome	Percent probability
Freeway driving	Never do it anymore, get rides or stay home	Freeway—4 exits—4 p.m.	50	2	Panic, have to stop	65
		Freeway—2 exits—5 p.m.	70	2	Panic, have to stop	70
Combo situations	All of above	Visualize 1st panic + drive	60	2	Panic, have to stop	80
		Visualize 1st panic + BART	70	1	Panic, have to get off	80
		Visualize 1st panic + freeway	70	2	Panic, have to stop	80
Going to the movies	Stay home, watch TV	Go to popular movie	65	4	Panic, have to leave	60
Eating out	Avoid	Go to popular restaurant	75	5	Panic, have to leave	80

Feared situation	Safety behaviors	Plan to stop safety behavior and to expose	SUDS 1–100	Value 1–5	Predicted worst-case outcome	Percent probability
Interoceptive panic sensations: being out of breath, hot, rapid heart rate, shaky muscles	Stop whatever I'm doing that seems to be causing it	Running in place—1 min.	75	2	Panic, have to stop	60
		Running in place—2 min.	85	2	Panic, have to stop	65
		Running + heavy coat—2 min.	95	2	Panic, have to stop	80
		Running, then driving	90	3	Panic, have to stop	90
		Very rapid breathing—1 min.	70	1	Panic, have to stop	80
		Very rapid breathing, then driving	85	2	Panic, have to stop	100
		Breathing through straw—1 min.	60	1	Panic, have to stop	65
		Half squat—2 min.	55	2	Panic, have to stop	65

For even more details on designing interoceptive exposures, see Appendix IV at the end of this book.

Specific Phobia—Sophia's Fear of Bees

Specific phobias can arise in connection to virtually any object or situation. Common phobias include insects, animals, heights, closed spaces, driving, injections and other medical procedures, public speaking, water, and many others. Developing items for a phobia inventory typically involves manipulating:

- **distance** from the feared object or situation, where the closer you get, the more you expect catastrophe

- **level of threat** such as how much time is spent near the feared object or in the feared situation. Or how dangerous the exposure feels—is it a picture of a snake or a real snake? How big is the snake? Is it in a cage? Will you touch it?

- **catastrophic images of worst-case outcomes** such as reading about someone who was bitten by a snake or imagining it.

The following inventory documents the exposure plan for Sophia, a professional gardener who was afraid of bees. She cared deeply about her job, as you'll see in her value ratings.

Sophia's Exposure Inventory Worksheet

Feared situation	Safety behaviors	Plan to stop safety behavior and to expose	SUDS 1–100	Value 1–5	Predicted worst-case outcome	Percent probability
Reading article about bees	Avoidance	Read article about someone attacked by bees	85	2	Too scared, put magazine down	90
		Hold a picture of a bee	40	1	Will drop it	60
		Look at picture of someone with multiple bee stings	80	2	Too scared, put picture down	90
Videos of bees	Avoidance	Looking at a video of bees on computer	50	1	Will turn it off	60
		Listening to recording of many bees buzzing	45	1	Will turn it off	65
Flower gardens with bees	Avoidance	Stand halfway to my dahlias (lots of bees) for 1 min.	65	3	Will be stung	60
		Stand halfway to my dahlias for 3 min.	75	3	Multiple stings	70

Feared situation	Safety behaviors	Plan to stop safety behavior and to expose	SUDS 1–100	Value 1–5	Predicted worst-case outcome	Percent probability
Flower gardens with bees	Avoidance	Stand next to dahlias for 30 sec.	80	3	Multiple stings	80
		Stand next to dahlias for 2 min.	90	3	Multiple stings	90
		Stand next to dahlias for 5 min.	95	3	Multiple stings	95
		Visit flower beds in Ms. Latham's yard	80	5	Will be stung	75
		Prune back a rosebush at Ms. Druery's	70	5	Multiple stings	75
Combos	Avoidance	Stand next to dahlias while reading bee attack article	100	3	Multiple stings	100
		Read bee attack article right before hoeing Ms. Latham's flower bed	90	5	Multiple stings	95

Specific Phobia—Stan's Fear of Needles

And here is another specific phobia inventory, this one by Stan, a newly diagnosed diabetic who was afraid of needles. As you can see from his value ratings, he had a strong value about staying healthy, which required him to learn to administer his own insulin injections.

Stan's Exposure Inventory Worksheet

Feared situation	Safety behaviors	Plan to stop safety behavior and to expose	SUDS 1–100	Value 1–5	Predicted worst-case outcome	Percent probability
Being around injection stuff— vials, syringes, etc.	Avoid, distract, ask for reassurance	Sit in doctor's waiting room	55	2	Leave immediately	60
		Look at picture of syringe	45	2	Stop, put it down	60
		Watch a video of someone getting a shot	50	2	Can't stand it, turn it off	90
		Watch nurse demonstrate injecting an orange	80	4	Leave immediately	80
		Smell alcohol on cotton ball	55	1	Stop immediately	60

Feared situation	Safety behaviors	Plan to stop safety behavior and to expose	SUDS 1–100	Value 1–5	Predicted worst-case outcome	Percent probability
Receiving an injection	Avoid, distract with chatter, look away	Visualize getting a painful shot	70	2	Cut off the images	65
		Visualize getting a shot, screaming and fainting	70	2	Cut off the images	70
		Nurse gives me an insulin shot in leg, watch it happen, don't look away	90	5	Scream, faint	85
Giving myself an insulin injection	Avoidance	Stick my finger with a pin	80	2	Can't do it	90
		Hold a syringe filled with saline	75	3	Stop, leave	90
		Give myself insulin shot in leg	100	5	Can't do it, faint	95

Post-Traumatic Stress Disorder (PTSD)
—Laura's Sexual Assault

Laura was the victim of a nighttime break-in during which she was slapped awake by her assailant and sexually assaulted in her bed. Since the attack, she's suffered flashbacks, surges of anxiety, and sadness, and she has an overwhelming fear of being alone at night.

Recovery from PTSD symptoms involves two very different kinds of exposure:

1. **Imagery exposure** that involves visualizing the event in detail. This can often be accomplished by making a recording lasting fifteen to thirty minutes describing each minute step of the trauma, including as much as possible about what happened emotionally, physically, and cognitively during the event.

2. **Situational exposure** to current fears that have been triggered by the trauma. For Laura, who must either spend the night at the home of friends or persuade friends to stay with her, the fear of being alone at night has become a serious problem. As you'll see, many items in her inventory are situational exposures designed to change the belief that she'll be attacked if she spends the night alone.

Laura has strong values about facing the pain in her life and maintaining her independence, as you'll see in her inventory.

Laura's Exposure Inventory Worksheet

Feared situation	Safety behaviors	Plan to stop safety behavior and to expose	SUDS 1–100	Value 1–5	Predicted worst-case outcome	Percent probability
Remembering the attack	Avoid, distract, mental rituals	Record the story of the attack on my phone—15 minutes long	85	5	Can't stand it, will have to stop	95
		Listen to 5 minutes of the recording on my phone, during which I describe everything that happened during the attack	80	5	Can't stand it, will have to stop	80
		Listen to 10 minutes of the recording	75	5	Can't stand it, will have to stop	75
		Listen to all 15 minutes of the recording	70	5	Can't stand it, will have to stop	75

Feared situation	Safety behaviors	Plan to stop safety behavior and to expose	SUDS 1–100	Value 1–5	Predicted worst-case outcome	Percent probability
Spending the night alone	Avoid, stay at friends' houses	Stay alone in hotel—1 night	70	4	Will be attacked	60
		Stay the night at a friend's house with no one there	70	3	Will be attacked	80
		Stay alone in hotel—2 nights	75	5	Will be attacked	70
		Listen to recording of attack + spend night in hotel	80	5	Will be attacked	75
		Stay alone at home until 10:00 p.m.	80	4	Will be attacked	70
		Listen to recording of attack + stay alone at home until midnight	85	5	Will be attacked	80
		Stay alone at home until midnight, then check into hotel	90	4	Will be attacked	80
		Spend night alone at home	100	5	Will be attacked	95

Post-Traumatic Stress Disorder (PTSD) —Aaron's Commuter Train Derailment

Three years ago, Aaron was in the second car of a high-speed commuter train when it left the tracks and plowed into a warehouse. Passengers flew through the air and there were four dead in Aaron's car. Survivors were trapped for more than an hour while rescuers and paramedics tried to reach them. While waiting for help, Aaron was in great pain with a broken leg and ribs.

As noted in Laura's case, PTSD must be treated with both imagery exposure (a recorded description of the event) and situational exposure for current, associated fears. In Aaron's case, he retained a morbid fear of trains, planes, and buses, and had been forced to quit his job because it required significant travel. Note that his valued exposures all involve increasing his ability to travel.

Aaron's Exposure Inventory Worksheet

Feared situation	Safety behaviors	Plan to stop safety behavior and to expose	SUDS 1–100	Value 1–5	Predicted worst-case outcome	Percent probability
Remembering the derailment	Avoiding, taking tranquilizers, drinking too much, distraction	Making an 18-minute recording of the accident—what I saw, heard, smelled, thought, and felt emotionally and physically	90	1	Have to quit	80
		Listen to recording once on day 1—no drinking, drugs, or distraction	85	1	Have to quit	80
		Listen to recording twice on day 2—no d, d, or d	80	1	Have to quit	80
		Listen to recording 3 times on day 3—no d, d, or d	65	1	Have to quit	70
		Listen to recording 4 times on day 4—no d, d, or d	60	1	Have to quit	70
		Listen to recording 5 times on day 5—no d, d, or d	50	1	Have to quit	65
		Read article about the derailment—no d, d, or d	50	1	Have to quit	65

Feared situation	Safety behaviors	Plan to stop safety behavior and to expose	SUDS 1–100	Value 1–5	Predicted worst-case outcome	Percent probability
Taking public transportation	Avoiding, distraction, tranquilizers	Trolley to zoo	45	2	Panic, get off	60
		Bus to Stonestown	45	2	Panic, get off	60
		Bus to Berkeley art museum	55	3	Panic, get off	75
		Train to Millbrae	70	2	Panic, get off, crash	80
		Train to San Jose	80	3	Panic, get off, crash	90
		Plane to LA to visit brother	55	4	Panic, want off, throw up, crash	60
Combos	Avoiding, distraction, tranquilizers	Listen to recording + train to Millbrae	85	2	Crash	75
		Listen to recording + train to San Jose	90	3	Crash	80
		Read about crash + train/bus to Yosemite	95	4	Crash	95

CHAPTER 6

The Anxiety Solution

The anxiety solution can be summarized as a deceptively simple two-step process:

1. Avoid what you usually do.

2. Do what you usually avoid.

Or in psychology jargon:

1. Stop your approach safety behavior.

2. Approach your avoidant safety behavior.

Or even more simply, in cowboy lingo:

1. Put down the bottle.

2. Get back on the horse.

If only it were that simple! Just to get ready, you've already had to do a lot of reading, a lot of intense pen and paper work that is scary in itself, a lot of learning, preparing, motivating, analyzing, ranking distress and values, and so on. And you have yet to actually put one of your plans into action.

But now all your work is going to pay off. In this chapter you will finally face and overcome your anxiety, turning off your old false alarms.

It's hard to face something you believe is very likely to harm you. And that's exactly what this treatment program is asking you to do. It would be understandable if you were thinking seriously about stopping right here, hoping to find some other way. But here's the problem: exposing yourself to what you fear is the *only* way to permanently surmount anxiety. And the exposure process offered here—though challenging—is faster and more effective than earlier therapies.

Other solutions don't work. Anxiety drugs are rarely a good option. They help only as long as you take them, and many cause chemical dependence. When you stop the drugs, the withdrawal or discontinuation syndrome can leave you feeling worse than before. Waiting and hoping sometimes seems like a solution because anxiety can spontaneously wax and wane. But the long-term trajectory for untreated anxiety disorders is that they usually get worse. Avoidance begets increased avoidance, and life becomes ever more restricted and closed in by fear. Another strategy, trying to get people to help you, reassure you, or protect you, also makes anxiety worse in the long run. Everything you do to feel safer brings momentary calm at best, before you get caught in the next round of anxiety.

Your belief that certain things will harm you cannot change without disconfirming experiences. When it comes to fear, everyone is from Missouri—we have to be shown. We have to experience directly the feared situation and see that we are unscathed by it. That's what will happen in this treatment program. It's hard, it requires courage, but it will set you free.

Fine-Tuning Your Exposure Inventory

Get out your Exposure Inventory Worksheet from the previous chapter. Before you put your various plans into action, you'll want to do some fine-tuning to guarantee maximum results.

Include only high percent probability items

Effective exposure depends on the *maximum discrepancy* between your predictions of harm and actual outcomes. Therefore, you should make sure that all your exposure items have probability percentages of over 60 percent. That way you will have maximum learning potential and the best opportunity to disconfirm your fears.

If an exposure item has less than a 60 percent probability of harm, extend the time spent in the exposure, plan to move closer to the feared situation, or combine it with another feared situation until the probability exceeds 60 percent.

Have a full range of probability percentages

Make sure that the exposure items on your inventory cover the full range of probability percentages, from 60 to 100 percent. Avoid large gaps of more than 10 percent—for example, where you have items at 60 percent and the next highest item is 80 percent. If need be, fill in these gaps with additional exposure items.

Include high-quality items only

Make sure that the plans you make for exposure to things you avoid meet these criteria:

- They are things you *want* to do, experiences you truly want to have, but have avoided due to fear.

- As many as possible should have higher-ranking numbers in the value column. They are things you value or need to do to have a complete or fulfilling life. Examples might include dating for someone with social anxiety, or getting on airplanes for a plane-phobic whose job requires travel, or schlepping one's children to school, soccer, and so on, for someone who fears driving.

- They are things that, when avoided, have affected your life in negative ways. For example, the fear of panic attacks may have kept you from meeting friends in restaurants, enjoying concerts, or taking public transportation. Social fears may have kept you from speaking up at work or participating in task groups. The fear of germs may have kept you from otherwise positive experiences that seemed to risk contagion.

- They are not actually, really dangerous. While frightening to you, they should be things that many people experience without apparent harm, things that are generally regarded as safe by most people. So no taking long walks at night in crime-ridden neighborhoods, no taunting vicious dogs, no driving over the speed limit in heavy traffic.

Expand types of exposure to include visualizations

Situational exposure, which involves being in or near something you expect to harm you, is not the only form of exposure. Imagery exposure is used to visualize frightening events from the past, to relive traumatic memories, or to "expose" yourself to situations that are not easily reproduced in real life. For example, it is not safe or practical to plan to encounter a real traffic accident or a poisonous spider, so you do it in your imagination.

Imagery exposures can also be attached to situational exposures in order to increase the expectation of a feared outcome, thus strengthening the disconfirming power of the exposure. In other words, when you deeply believe something bad will happen, and it doesn't, you start to disconnect the exposure experience from the idea that you'll be harmed. For example, you might precede a freeway driving exposure with an image of a traffic accident, thus increasing your expectation of harm.

Reading about scary things related to a feared situation, just before an exposure, can also make the exposure more effective. By intensifying the expectation of harm, an outcome in which no harm comes to you helps you learn that the exposure stimulus isn't dangerous.

Consider adding interoceptive exposure

This is exposure to physical sensations that you identify with fear and danger, such as being out of breath, being hot, having an elevated heart rate, having shaky muscles, and so on. Interoceptive exposure was covered in the previous chapter, under panic disorder. There's also more information in appendix IV at the end of this book.

• *Example: Harry's Fine-Tuning*

Harry struggled with the fear of panicking in public places. When he got to this stage in his treatment of his panic disorder, his exposure inventory was a little skimpy. It looked like this:

Harry's Exposure Inventory Worksheet #1

Feared situation	Safety behaviors	Plan to stop safety behavior and to expose	SUDS 1–100	Value 1–5	Predicted worst-case outcome	Percent probability
Eating out	Avoid	Order tea in diner	50	2	Will have a panic attack, have to leave, be incapacitated for hours	45
		Eat lunch at nice restaurant with a friend	85	4	All of the above, plus friend will be angry	90
		Take girlfriend out to eat	75	5	All of the above, plus she will be angry for days	80
Being outside, away from home	Avoid, check and recheck for phone and keys, Take own car	Take 1-mile walk along river	60	4	Will panic, feel weak, barely make it home	50
		Take bus to work	80	4	Will panic, have to call a friend to take me home	80
Having elevated heart rate, feeling hot and out of breath	Have stopped going to gym	30 minutes in gym, getting hot, sweaty	80	4	Have to leave, feel incapacitated all day	80

Harry looked at his probability percentages and realized that ordering tea in the diner and taking a one-mile walk were under 60 percent. So he planned to also order a sandwich and increased the walk to two miles, raising the probability percentages to 60 and 65 percent respectively.

He also noticed that he didn't have a really challenging situation in which the probability percentage reached 100 percent, so he added a weekend trip that his girlfriend had always wanted to take. He also added a couple of mid-range exposures to different feared situations to flesh out his inventory. One of them, going to popular movies, was something he really used to like to do, a high-value exposure.

Harry added a visualization of being lost in a strange city, late at night, and running out of gas. It was a situation he greatly feared, but he couldn't figure out how to arrange it in real life. He also added some imagery exposure to his plan to take a two-mile walk along the river. While walking, he would visualize the time he had his first panic attack, on a hike with a former girlfriend.

Harry beefed up his plan to experience his panic sensations at the gym by adding a heavy sweatshirt and a visit to the sauna to address his fear of feeling hot. He also increased the time exercising in order to experience longer elevations of his heart and breath rate.

The final version of Harry's inventory looked like this:

Harry's Exposure Inventory Worksheet #2

Feared situation	Safety behaviors	Plan to stop safety behavior and to expose	SUDS 1–100	Value 1–5	Predicted worst-case outcome	Percent probability
Eating out in a restaurant	Avoid, eat at home, call for delivery	Order tea and sandwich in diner, stay 30 minutes	50	3	Will have a panic attack, have to leave, be incapacitated for hours	60
		Eat lunch at nice restaurant with a friend	85	4	All of the above, plus friend will be angry	90
		Take girlfriend out to eat	75	5	All of the above, plus she will be angry for days	80
Going to movies	Just don't do it anymore	Go to crowded movie with girlfriend, sit in the middle of a row	70	3	Will feel so claustrophobic that I'll have to leave early	85
Remembering first panic attack	Distraction	Visualize first panic attack for 1 min., then 2, then 3 min.	60	2	Won't last, will have to stop visualization	85

Feared situation	Safety behaviors	Plan to stop safety behavior and to expose	SUDS 1–100	Value 1–5	Predicted worst-case outcome	Percent probability
Being outdoors or out of town, far away from home	Avoid, check and recheck for phone, keys, etc.	Take 2-mile walk along river after imagining the time I had a panic attack on a hike	65	4	Will panic, feel weak, barely make it home	65
	Always drive my own car, stay close to home	Take bus to work	75	3	Will panic, have to call a friend to take me home	70
		Walk in Muir Woods with girlfriend	85	5	Panic will make me cut it short	75
		Go on weekend trip with girlfriend to Clear Lake	95	5	I'll freak out, have to cut trip short and have her drive me home.	100
Feeling hot, panting, heart racing	Have stopped working out	10 min. in sauna at gym, wearing sweatshirt, then 20 min. on treadmill, getting hot, sweaty, out of breath. Then increase to 35 min.	80	6	Will panic and have to leave, feel incapacitated all day	80
Driving in strange city, getting lost	Stay close to home, fill up tank frequently	Visualize for 15 min. being lost in Chicago, late at night, bad neighborhood, and running out of gas	100	4	Won't be able to finish the visualization, will have to stop	95

Guidelines for Effective Exposures

These guidelines will help you solve your anxiety problem as quickly and thoroughly as possible. When you begin to experience your exposure situations in real life, review this section to make sure you are maximizing your chances of success.

How to Choose Your First Exposure

Start small. Make your first exposure an item that has the lowest SUDS in your inventory. It's best to start with something that doesn't push your fear all the way to the top. Later you can randomize exposures, but let this first one be relatively easy.

Choosing the Next Exposure: Random or Gradual Sequence?

Until recently, gradual or hierarchical exposure has been the gold standard for treating anxiety. You face your fear in small, graduated steps, a hierarchy from the least to the most feared item. This standard was based on the concept of habituation: you experience a low-level anxiety stimulus and stay in the situation until there is full desensitization and you feel no more fear. For example, people afraid of freeways might stand on the side of the road and watch an on ramp for half an hour. Then they would move up to being a passenger in the slow lane for a quarter mile. Eventually they'd work up to driving for real on the freeway. It took a long time and sometimes there were significant setbacks, when anxiety would suddenly flair up and they would have to break the exposure into smaller steps.

A better way to do exposure has since been discovered (Craske et al., 2014) that takes less time and produces more lasting results, fewer relapses, and a profoundly positive change in your relationship to anxiety. It is called *inhibitory learning*. Instead of relying exclusively on habituation, which can so easily unravel and reverse, inhibitory learning helps you learn that *the things you fear will not happen*. This shift in your catastrophic beliefs—that terrible things will occur if you get on an elevator, touch a bathroom doorknob, say hello to a stranger, go far from home, or whatnot—is a game changer that can permanently liberate you from a life of anxiety. Instead of believing that the worst will happen, you will have learned that there is *no relationship between the old feared stimulus and disaster.*

That's why exposures in this program always include a worst-case prediction and your estimate of the percent probability of the prediction coming true. After each exposure, you get a chance to learn about the *actual* dangerousness of things you fear.

The inhibitory learning model breaks with exposure traditions in other ways. It replaces the old hierarchical exposure approach with random exposures. Instead of using a hierarchy in which you expose yourself stepwise up a ladder of increasingly fearful situations, you do exposures in a deliberately random order, mixing situations that cause you varying levels of distress (SUDS). This is a faster way to learn that your predictions of catastrophe will not come true.

So, after starting with your lowest SUDS item, jump to one with significantly higher SUDS, and a higher percent probability of harm. As you expose yourself to items with different SUDS levels—some lower, some higher—it serves to better disconfirm your expectation that bad things will happen. Keep jumping around your inventory by asking the questions "What do I need to learn next?" and "What avoided experience do I need to face next?"

> Special note: Randomizing exposures instead of gradually progressing from lower to higher fear-evoking items is challenging. We strongly suggest you do this because treatment results are more rapid and complete. However, some people find that random exposures present a level of fear and difficulty that is too challenging to face. If, after attempting random exposures, you feel too anxious to go on, we suggest you reorder your inventory as a hierarchy, with items arranged from the lowest to highest SUDS rating. Work up the hierarchy gradually, attempting an exposure to the next-highest item *only* after learning to face the one below it.

Here are the other general rules to keep in mind as you create your inventory:

Use high-value exposures

When taking on higher SUDS items with more challenging fear levels, initially select exposures that also have *higher value ratings*. So while the exposure may be more scary, it is also something you want to do—it really matters to you. If you think back to Harry's inventory, for example, high-value items like going to the gym were also quite frightening (high SUDS).

Vary exposure contexts

This means, in Harry's case, that if he does an exercise exposure in the gym, the next exposure should be in a different setting—a brisk walk by the river, or on the crowded streets downtown. Keep altering where, how, and with whom you do certain exposures so you'll learn to face the fear in multiple contexts.

Pay attention during exposure

During exposure, fully observe your emotions, body sensations, and thoughts. Notice the full range of your experience. In your mind, try to name the feelings you have, and watch as they may shift and change during the exposure. Do nothing to avoid or numb your feelings. Don't try to reassure yourself, use coping thoughts, or try to control your fear in any way. In other words, do nothing to feel safer.

Stay aware of the exposure experience itself. For example, if you are exposing to heights, you might try to focus on objects below you, noticing how far away they seem. If you are exposing to a social anxiety, it would be helpful to observe people's tone of voice and facial expressions as they speak to you.

Stay in the exposure long enough

Long enough means the full length of time you planned. Anything less won't fully disconfirm your prediction of the worst-case outcome. If you can't last the whole time, you'll have to break up the exposure into two or more sessions in which you can stay for the whole time. Alter your inventory accordingly as you go along.

Try to stay in the exposure or repeat it until your *expectation* (percent probability) that the feared outcome will occur has dropped significantly. It doesn't matter whether your actual fear level has gone down—only that your expectation of harm has decreased. If you thought you'd need to expose yourself to a scary situation for an hour, but your expectation of disaster drops to 10 percent after fifteen minutes, you've accomplished your goal and you can stop.

Combine exposures

Once you have some successful exposures under your belt, you can try combining exposures. You can combine two situational exposures, or pair a situational exposure with imagery or interoceptive exposure. Combined exposures result in something called *deepened extinction*—a more profound violation of your expectation of harm, and something associated with better treatment outcomes. But when you combine situational exposures, make sure you have already done at least one of them already.

Evaluate your results after each exposure

After each exposure, fill out one of the Results Tracker worksheets provided later in the chapter. It gives you plenty of room to answer four important questions:

1. Did the feared result happen—yes or no?

2. What happened instead?

3. How do you rate the percent probability of the feared outcome now?

4. What did you learn from the exposure?

Now Do It

You are ready. Grab your fine-tuned Exposure Inventory Worksheet, pick out your first exposure experience, and *go out and do it*. Work through your list of exposures systematically, following the guidelines and evaluating each exposure upon completion.

• *Example: Harry's Exposure Process*

Harry's first exposure was to his inventory item with the lowest SUDS—going to the diner to order tea and a sandwich. He had no panic attack and stayed for 40 minutes, finishing every crumb and drop. Twenty minutes into the experience he realized that his expectation of a disastrous attack had declined to nearly zero percent. While he finished his meal he pulled out his Results Tracker and wrote up his experience, rating the probability of his worst-case outcome happening as 4 percent.

Harry didn't decide on the order of his exposures in advance. Instead, he kept asking these questions: (1) "What do I need to learn next?" (2) "What avoided experience do I need to face next?" (3) "How can I achieve maximum violation of my predicted outcomes (percent probability that what I fear will actually happen)?"

For his second exposure, Harry skipped eating out with a friend and jumped right to having dinner with his girlfriend at her favorite restaurant. He was combining a high-fear with a high-value experience. Though a slow, sit-down meal was scary (he rated an 80 percent chance of panic), showing his girlfriend a good time was very important to him. They spent most of their nights at home, and she chafed at the ways his life had become constricted.

While they waited to give their order, Harry's heart started to pound. He felt hot and his breath rate climbed. Harry just observed his experience moment by moment, feeling his heart and breath, having the thought, *Here we go*, meaning a panic was imminent. He looked at the waiters with their trays; he listened to the murmur of conversation. Despite the fear, he was determined to stay for the full meal, and he did. Later that night, Harry wrote in his Results Tracker that he had panicked, but it lasted only a minute or two. He didn't have to run home, and his girlfriend—best of all—had a good time on their dinner date. When he re-rated the percent probability that he would panic and have to leave a restaurant, it was down to 20 percent.

Harry decided to take on something very different for his next exposure item. He went to the gym for 30 minutes of sauna and treadmill. He had rated the likelihood of panic at 80 percent, and assumed he'd be forced to leave before the allotted time. To his surprise, Harry discovered that his heart could race and he could perspire and be out of breath, and yet not panic. He was actually starting to get used to these sensations. The next day he went to the gym to work out like he used to.

Harry asked the question, "What do I need to do next?" and scanned his inventory. Intuitively, it occurred to him that he needed to face the fear associated with his original panic attack. So he visualized the scene on the hiking trail for 1, then 2, then 3 minutes. Though he expected an 85 percent chance of panic, his heart raced without further symptoms, and the percent probability went down to 5 percent on his testing worksheet.

Next, Harry visualized his first panic just before a hike by the river, and later combined the same visualization with a movie date with his girlfriend. Though Harry sometimes had brief panic symptoms, none of them incapacitated him or forced a return home. He was beginning to believe no great harm would come to him for the items he'd already tested.

Harry tried other exposure contexts—walking briskly on the crowded downtown streets, and hiking with his girlfriend in Muir Woods. He continued to vary items in terms of fear intensity and expectation of harm. Whenever possible, he combined high SUDS items with things he wanted to do and greatly valued. While these high SUDS items were scary, they were also experiences he felt very motivated to face.

During each exposure, Harry observed both his internal feelings and the external sensations. He watched all that went on without resisting, coping, or distracting from the exposure. And, with each successful exposure, he felt more and more convinced that the things he'd avoided for so long would not hurt him.

Harry got to where he could "freestyle" exposures that were not planned out on his inventory. He started taking the subway to work sometimes, or taking the bus partway and walking the rest. He also chose to walk for various periods on the beach, in an empty area of a big park, and on several new hiking trails. He even decided to take a two-hour hike with a group of outdoor enthusiasts at work. His girlfriend pointed out to him that what he called "freestyling" other people called "living your life."

Results Tracker

Here is the worksheet for tracking your results after each exposure, followed by an explanation of how to answer each of the four questions, and examples of how others have used the Results Tracker. (This worksheet is also available for download at http://www.newharbinger .com/34749.)

Results Tracker

Exposure:
Predicted worst-case outcome:
1. **Did the worst-case outcome happen?** _____ Yes _____ No
2. **What happened instead?**
3. **Percent probability:** Before: _____ After: _____
4. **What did you learn from the exposure?**
5. **SUDS 1–100:** Before: _____ After: _____

Exposure

Write out what you did in detail and how you followed your plan for exposing yourself to the feared situation without using any of your preferred safety behaviors.

Predicted Worst-Case Outcome

Write down the worse-case scenario of what you think will happen.

Did the Worst-Case Outcome Happen?

This is a simple "yes" or "no" evaluation of what happened. Either the harm you predicted occurred, or it did not. Put an "x" next to either yes or no on the Results Tracker. Because predictions should describe observable outcomes—either events or behaviors—the answer to this question should reflect actual events, rather than feelings or impressions.

What Happened Instead?

Describe exactly what happened. What behaviors did you or others display, either during or right after the exposure? Did you follow your plan exactly, or were there differences? If the worst-case outcome you predicted didn't occur, what events did you observe during the test? As much as possible, be a personal scientist and describe the exposure outcome objectively.

An example would be a man who feared germs. Unless he washed thoroughly for half an hour after touching a series of knobs in a bus station, he predicted, he would grow very ill within three days. Here's how he described what happened: "A day after the doorknob test, I felt a little tired, not quite my usual energy. Day two I was okay, but I blew my nose a few times. Day three I was okay, no noticeable symptoms. I gave myself an extra day, but even on day four I felt pretty healthy. I don't have any symptoms of illness."

Percent Probability

Write down the percent probability for the worst-case outcome that you had before the exposure, and the percent probability for the worst-case outcome now, after the exposure experiment.

What Did You Learn from the Exposure?

This is the time to make sense of your experiment. How do you explain the outcomes? If the predicted harm didn't occur—as is almost universally the case—what does that tell you about the dangerousness of this experience? Did anything surprise you? How likely does the predicted harm seem now—in terms of percent probability?

For example, a woman predicted having a panic attack and becoming incapacitated and unable to drive if she attempted to cross the Golden Gate Bridge. She wrote this summary of her learning on her Results Tracker: "I was anxious. My heart rate was way up. It was pounding. And I felt light-headed like I get. I was 'panicky' but not in full panic. I was able to drive okay, which surprised me. I was able to react appropriately to traffic, and even get out of the way of a car that was merging into my lane. I learned I can get anxious without having a panic attack, and I can drive okay even if my heart is racing. I stay functional. Percent probability that I won't be able to drive and have to stop on the bridge: 40 percent."

SUDS 1–100

Record the SUDS from your Exposure Inventory Worksheet, and the SUDS you felt just as you ended the exposure. This is probably the least important information on the Results Tracker, because the object of exposure is not necessarily to reduce your SUDS. However, it can be interesting to compare post-exposure SUDS to the SUDS level you expected for this experience in your inventory.

• *Example: Obsessive-Compulsive Disorder*

After reading about a child who ran into the street and was killed by a car, Aaron could hardly get the thought out of his mind, especially while driving. He imagined that small children could run out and fall under his wheels and he might not even know it. He began driving only short distances, retracing the whole route at least once to see if he hit anyone without noticing. He avoided driving anywhere near schools and playgrounds, and generally would not travel more than fifteen miles per hour. Here is one of his Result Trackers:

Aaron's Results Tracker: Fear of Doing Harm

Exposure: *Drive 22 miles to visit mother after Googling and reading articles about children being hit by cars. No retracing route.*

Predicted worst-case outcome: *I will hit a child while I drive and read about it in the newspaper the next day.*

1. Did the worst-case outcome happen? _____ Yes ___X___ No

2. What happened instead? *There were no newspaper reports of children who were victims of a hit and run. There was an accident where a child was hurt inside a car, but that's all. I was also worried, I'll admit it now, that I'd be so scared I'd have to retrace my route. But I forced myself to park and ring my mother's bell.*

3. Percent probability: Before: ___80___ After: ___60___

4. What did you learn from the exposure? *I learned that I can drive at a moderate speed and a moderate distance without hitting a child, at least this time.*

5. SUDS 1–100: Before: ___95___ After: ___75___

• *Example Panic Disorder*

Beth's first panic attack occurred while she was driving over a high suspension bridge. She had just left her father's funeral and was on her way home. It was so horrible that she was determined never to let it happen again. Over the next few days she vigilantly watched for the first physiological signs—the feeling that she couldn't catch her breath, dizziness, and a pounding heart. But despite her efforts, the panic returned in several settings—such as in a restaurant, on a bus, and walking to work. More and more she tried to avoid situations in which she'd previously panicked. But it didn't work. The frequency of her attacks went from once a month to twice a week. Here are the results of her first exposure:

Beth's Results Tracker: Panic

Exposure: *Run in place for 2 minutes until I'm out of breath and my heart is pounding.*

Predicted worst-case outcome: *I'll get so panicked that I can't stand it and will have to stop early. I'll be too upset to do anything the rest of the day.*

1. Did the worst-case outcome happen? _____ Yes ___X___ No

2. What happened instead? *I got winded and my heart was racing. But I made it through the full 2 minutes. I was able to do the bills after, and go over and visit Joan that night. I was anxious, but I got though the exercise and could still function.*

3. Percent probability: Before: ___95___ After: ___60___

4. What did you learn from the exposure? *I learned that I could stand the feeling of being out of breath and having my heart pound. The feeling doesn't incapacitate me. I can carry on with my life.*

5. SUDS 1–100: Before: ___90___ After: ___50___

• *Example: Specific Phobia*

Janice was afraid of heights. It began at age eleven, when her brother encouraged her to climb a water tower, then left her up there, terrified to climb back down the ladder. While completing a degree in structural engineering, Janice landed an internship with a major construction firm. Part of her job was going to be inspecting construction sites, which often involved working in tall, partially completed buildings. Moving forward with her career required that Janice overcome her acrophobia.

Janice's Results Tracker: Acrophobia

Exposure: *Go with friend to third floor of building under construction.*

Predicted worst-case outcome: *I will slide, fall, or jump off the edge of the open floor. Something will pull or compel me to fall.*

1. Did the worst-case outcome happen? _____ Yes ___X___ No

2. What happened instead? *I'm alive and uninjured—I'd be dead if I'd fallen. I felt a little dizzy up there. I had a picture in my mind of the floor tilting and me sliding off. And then—like I'd seen in a movie—I imagined myself running full-out over the edge. But none of those things happened.*

3. Percent probability: Before: ___70___ After: ___40___

4. What did you learn from the exposure? *That having pictures in my mind of horrible things doesn't make them happen. That I'm not going to fall if I'm 10 feet from the edge, no matter what story I'm on.*

5. SUDS 1–100: Before: ___80___ After: ___60___

• *Example: Post-Traumatic Stress Disorder*

Arturo was attacked at an ATM at night. Three men hit him, one with a wrench. While half-conscious, he felt them meticulously go through his pockets and take everything of value. Six months after the assault Arturo was experiencing flashbacks, mood swings, and nightmares. He had become extremely fearful of going out at night and walking near groups of men, even on safe, well-traveled streets.

Arturo's Results Tracker: Fear of Assault

Exposure: *Walk down Market Street between Sixth and New Montgomery (a busy commercial area) at 8 p.m.*

Predicted worst-case outcome: *I'll be attacked and beaten on the street.*

---

1. Did the worst-case outcome happen? _____ Yes ____X____ No

---

2. What happened instead? *I got all the way to New Montgomery and nobody even seemed to notice me, let alone make a move toward me. I was nervous at first, although that got better. I did the visualization of my mugging in a coffee shop. I'd done it before, so it didn't scare me as much as I thought. I felt like I could face the walk back, so I did.*

---

3. Percent probability: Before: ____75____ After: ____50____

---

4. What did you learn from the exposure? *I learned that I can probably walk down Market Street without anyone bothering me and that expecting something to happen doesn't mean it will. I have more ability to face things than I thought.*

---

5. SUDS 1–100: Before: ____80____ After: ____50____

When Exposure Ends

After you have worked through your inventory, what happens when you encounter some of those same feared situations again? Your anxiety or subjective units of distress (SUDS) will be *significantly reduced*. The anxiety is unlikely to completely disappear, but that's not the point of this treatment. The point of the treatment is to significantly reduce your anxiety, and the time when the formal exposure process ends is when you can *do all the things you used to avoid.*

No one's life is free of anxiety. We all have fears. But the goal is to live life fully—free to do the things that matter to you—even if sometimes the alarm goes off.

Harry stopped planning exposures when he could do all the things in his inventory that mattered to him. Sometimes he felt twinges of the old anxiety, and there were situations in which the thought occurred to him that he might panic. But he had learned one thing: the old symptoms couldn't hurt or incapacitate him. He could do everything he wanted to do.

CHAPTER 7

You Can Face Fear

This is the first of four chapters that teach what we consider auxiliary skills. This one is about correctly assessing your ability to cope with threats. The next chapter is about using a technique called defusion to reduce worry and rumination. Chapter 9 shows how to more accurately assess dangers and threats. And chapter 10 teaches how to increase your distress tolerance.

A Warning

As you have learned so far, the royal road to anxiety management is *exposure*. The first half of this book has taught you how to assess your anxiety, stop safety behaviors, design systematic exposure experiences, and work through them in real life. *The real-life exposure experiences are the heart of this book.* If you have not conscientiously done the exercises in the previous six chapters, *we urge you to go back and do them.* It's the fastest and surest way to feel better.

That said, this and the next three chapters contain instructions for cognitive behavioral skills that can help you manage your anxiety, especially for situations in which exposure is not possible or feasible at the moment.

Your Ability to Cope

In chapter 2, you learned about the alarm response that human beings evolved to handle threats effectively and survive. To review, this alarm response has four steps:

1. *Perception of threat*—the alarm sounds.

2. *Appraisal of threat*—you assess how serious the danger is and whether you have the resources to cope.

3. *Physiological and emotional responses*—you experience a cascade of physical sensations preparing you to deal with danger (tightened muscles; adrenaline-mediated changes in digestion, heart rate, and breathing) and the emotion of fear/anxiety.

4. *Behavioral response*—you try to avoid the threat, or you do something to feel safer.

Chapter 2 went on to explain that how you accomplish the second step, *appraisal of threat*, has a lot to do with how much fear you experience. Part of appraising threat is assessing your ability to cope with the threat. If you think that you have no ability to cope, then any threat, even the most minor, becomes overwhelming.

This chapter teaches you to face fear by highlighting your ability to cope. You will start by writing a "coping memoir." In your coping memoir you will tell the story of difficult situations you've experienced in the past, and how you survived them. By mining your past for examples of how you have already coped, you will expand your thinking beyond the narrow scope of your usual anxious thoughts, allowing you to face your fears more calmly.

After you compose your coping memoir, you will use it to compose a set of coping thoughts. Coping thoughts are short statements that you can use in the future, when you face anxiety-provoking situations, to remind yourself of your ability to cope.

Finally, you will imagine your worst-case scenario—what you are most afraid might happen in the future. You will succinctly describe the disaster you fear, making it as bad as it can possibly be. Then you will draft a worst-case coping plan instead of spiraling down into a pit of worry and fear. Your coping plan is a detailed list of what you would do to cope with disaster, broken down into how you would act, feel, think, speak, and interact with others in your worst-case scenario. This is a powerful exercise that teaches you the value of thinking flexibly, realistically, and positively about the future.

The Gap Between Fear and Reality

In chapter 6 you exposed yourself to experiences and situations you fear. It's likely that you discovered a significant gap between how well you expected to cope and how well you actually did cope. This gap between your fearful expectations and the reality of your coping experience is the opening that you need to change your beliefs, become more flexible in your thinking, and face your fears with more confidence.

Your lack of confidence in your coping ability is based upon habitual, recurring, overly cautious thoughts. These thoughts reinforce your negative beliefs about yourself, about certain scary situations, or about the future in general:

I'll never be good enough.

I always screw up.

I can't face speaking in front of a group.

If I drive that highway, a truck is going to hit me head on.

Something bad is bound to happen.

Don't blame yourself. Your mind is hardwired by thousands of years of evolution to protect you from harm. Your negative expectations and elevated level of anxiety are a result of the natural alarm response that you share with all the other humans who have ever lived. Your alarm response is just overdeveloped. It needs to be toned down, tempered by more flexible, realistic, and confident thoughts of how you have coped in the past.

Your goal in this chapter is to expand your perception beyond the overly negative outcomes you habitually foresee, to include your memories of successful coping in the past. Your goal is to enlarge and inhabit the gap between fear and reality.

Learning from Exposure

You can learn a lot about your coping abilities from your experiences with exposure in chapter 6. Review your Exposure Inventory Worksheet and recall how you acted and felt when you actually exposed yourself to the people, places, and experiences you fear.

What did it feel like as you decided on the first exposure to experience? What automatic predictions did you make? What thoughts went through your mind as you entered into the experience, passed through it, and came out the other side? What did you do and feel that surprised you? Your feelings, thoughts, and actions are the raw material of your coping abilities. Use the following worksheet to craft this raw material into some concrete insights about your coping strategies and abilities. (A downloadable version of this worksheet is available at http://www.newharbinger.com/34749.)

In the first column, briefly describe one of your exposure sessions, and rate your Subjective Units of Distress (1 for zero distress to 10 for maximum distress). In the next column, describe all the ways you coped with the experience: what you did, what you said to yourself, how you handled the fear as it rose and fell in intensity. Then rate your SUDS after the experience.

Learning Coping from Exposure Worksheet

Exposure experience	SUDS: Before	How I coped	SUDS: After

Describe and rate several of your exposure experiences, covering a variety of situations and fears. When Akram filled out this worksheet, one of his exposure experiences was going into a government office to pick up an application for a green card. This exposure combined his fear of having a panic attack in a public place and having to interact with authority figures:

Akram's Learning Coping from Exposure Worksheet

Exposure experience	SUDS: Before	How I coped	SUDS: After
I took the bus downtown and went to the Federal Building, talked to the information person in the lobby, went up in the elevator, found the right office, and asked the clerk for the paperwork. At each step I felt scared, afraid I'd have a panic attack or be challenged by someone in authority. Wanted to run away. Wanted to say, "Never mind, it's not important."	5–9	I felt the fear peak and subside, peak and subside, like waves. Kept thinking, *Just do one thing at a time.* Focused on what I physically had to do to keep on going. Focused on my values, that a green card was important to me, so I didn't let myself down.	3

Your Coping Memoir

Even if you are relatively young, you have undoubtedly faced some challenging situations in the past and coped with them successfully. It's very helpful to remind yourself that you are still alive today because of your successful coping in the past. It is well worth it to spend some time composing a brief coping memoir right now. In the following worksheet, tell the story of five episodes from your life, five challenges that you have had to cope with in the past.

In the first column, write down a situation that you found very challenging. It can be a social situation, a health crisis, a financial reversal, an accident, or something that happened in your family or community. Go into as much detail as you can. Include not only what happened but also how you felt, what other people said and did that made it worse, your thoughts and feelings at the time, and your actions and reactions as events unfolded.

In the second column indicate your Subjective Unit's of Distress (SUDS)—a number from 1 to 10, with 1 indicating almost no distress, up to 10 indicating the most distress you could possibly feel.

In the third column, write down how you coped: what you did, said, felt, and thought that helped you to cope with the situation. Ask yourself these two questions:

- How did I cope with the situation?

- How did I cope with the fear itself?

Finally, in the last column, rate the subjective distress you felt after coping. Notice how much your anxiety and other feelings decreased after you coped with the situation.

My Coping Memoir

Challenging situation	SUDS: Before	How I coped	SUDS: After

If you're like most people, your life has not been free of challenges. Some of them may have taxed you to your limit. And yet you have survived. You are still here, still alive to cope and survive another day. And most likely, what you did to cope in the past helped lower your feelings of distress.

• *Example: Amara*

Amara was afraid of many things: snakes, spiders, dark holes, sudden noises, traffic, bridges, tunnels, big trucks, and knives. She worried about her daughter's health and safety in a marginal neighborhood, her son's drug problem, and her own finances. Her best friend, Betsy, described her as a "nervous wreck at the best of times." And yet Amara had somehow managed to survive for fifty-eight years on a planet beset with dangers on every side. How was that possible? Here is her coping memoir:

Amara's Coping Memoir

Challenging situation	SUDS: Before	How I coped	SUDS: After
When I was a kid my dad died and we had to move from our nice suburban house into a horrible Detroit apartment. Roaches, loud neighbors, cold concrete, dirt. I cried myself to sleep.	9	At first I was devastated, but when I saw how devastated Mom was, I made an effort to be more upbeat and complain less. We sprayed for the roaches and hung heavy drapes and turned the TV up loud. We survived by setting aside the fear and dealing with concrete problems one at a time.	6
Changed to a scary inner-city school in fifth grade, bigger and tougher than my old school. Felt in the crosshairs all the time.	7	I hid out in the library and later with the school newspaper staff. Found my people and my safe places. Discovered the world of books. The fear couldn't follow me into books.	4

Husband left me with two teenage kids and no money, almost no skills. Lonely and terrified. Drinking a lot. Mom blamed me.	8	Managed to keep the house, held down two jobs, got the kids through high school alive. Dealt with fear the wrong way, with wine. And the right way, with action.	4
Son was arrested for selling pot. I was ashamed, freaked out, furious. He was defiant and so stupid.	6	Managed to pay the lawyer, talk the judge into suspended sentence, get him into counseling. Saw that fear kept me from being strong, and I had to be strong because he was so weak then.	3
Daughter assaulted last summer at the bus stop. Cops called me and I fell on the floor in fear. Could hardly drive to the hospital.	9	Drove her to and from work for three weeks until she was strong enough to face taking the bus again. I'm still ready and able to support her as she needs it. Need to show an example of being scared but carrying on.	6

Amara tended to forget that she was actually strong and competent in the face of real-life challenges, especially when they involved protecting and helping her family. She kept a copy of her coping memoir on her computer desktop and a printout in her purse, as a reminder.

Your Coping Thoughts

Review the coping memoir you just wrote, plus your records from chapters 2 through 6, in which you wrote about your anxiety and exposure experiences. This material is full of good ideas for coping thoughts.

Coping thoughts are short, positive self-statements that remind you of your ability to cope. Here are some examples of good coping thoughts:

- *It's okay to make a mistake.*

- *I can be satisfied with my best effort.*

- *I've gotten through this before.*

- *I can do it.*

- *Just breathe deeply and relax.*

- *I know how to do this.*

- *Just hang in there until the end.*

Use the spaces below to write your coping thoughts in your own words. Remember to compose thoughts that address both what you can do to face challenging situations and what you can do to face the fear itself. (A downloadable version of this worksheet is available at http://www.newharbinger.com/34749.)

Coping Thoughts

My coping thoughts for facing challenging situations

My coping thoughts for facing fear itself

As an example, here are Amara's coping thoughts, based largely on her coping memoir:

Amara's Coping Thoughts

My coping thoughts for facing challenging situations
I can deal with one thing at a time.
Keep moving forward, taking action.
It will be over soon.
I am strong for my family.
My coping thoughts for facing fear itself
I can shut my eyes for a moment, breathe deeply, and imagine my safe place.
The fear comes in waves—it always recedes eventually.
I have carried on before when I was scared.

Worst-Case Coping Plan

If what you fear actually were to happen, you assume that you could not cope with it. You have images of yourself falling apart completely, succumbing to a total catastrophe. You say to yourself, "I couldn't stand it if X happens."

But what if the worst possible "X" happens? What exactly would it look like? Since people do survive all sorts of horrible experiences every day, and since it is literally impossible to "fall apart," what would you actually do in your worst-case scenario? To find out, create a worst-case coping plan.

Make a couple of copies of the following worksheet, so that you can use this exercise to make plans for all the things you fear. (A downloadable version of the worksheet is available at http://www.newharbinger.com/34749.) Then assume that the worst has happened—a cancer diagnosis, losing your job, a loved one dying, the end of your relationship—one of the main disasters you tend to worry about. Write it down on the first line of one of your worksheet copies.

Now imagine how you might cope with this eventuality. Think in terms of four kinds of coping:

- **Behavioral coping.** What actions would you take? If you lost your job, how would you go about looking for another one? What would be your financial resources? How would you cut expenses and/or raise extra cash? If you faced a medical emergency, what would you do to get a second opinion, explore treatment options, change your environment or lifestyle?

- **Emotional coping.** Next, move on to how you would deal with all the feelings that would come up. Write out how you would deal with your anxiety, anger, or depression by confronting your fears, enduring difficult situations, and persisting through painful feelings. Review your coping memoir and coping thoughts for other ways you can cope emotionally.

- **Cognitive coping.** Here is where you can use the coping thoughts you developed in the preceding section. Write them down here, as they apply to this worst-case scenario.

- **Interpersonal coping.** Who could help? What family members, friends, or colleagues could you call on for assistance? Write their names here and jot a note about how you would ask them for help.

Coping Plan Worksheet

Worst-case scenario: _____

_____

_____

_____

Behavioral coping: _____

_____

_____

_____

Emotional coping: _____

_____

_____

_____

Cognitive coping: _____

_____

_____

_____

Interpersonal coping: _____

_____

_____

_____

Susanna was a student at a junior college, the first in her family to go to college. She had to pass her math final in order to get her associate's degree and go on to a four-year college. With her history of poor performance on science and math tests, and her worries about failure and letting her family down, she needed to have a coping plan.

Susanna's Coping Plan Worksheet

Worst-case scenario: *I'll stay up all night studying, be tired and spacey for the test. Too nervous to eat breakfast, I'll feel panicky with a stomachache and shaky hands. When I get to the hard equations on the test, my mind will go blank and I'll just stare at the page. I'll hand in an incomplete test and get an F.*

Behavioral coping: *I'll study until 1 a.m., have a piece of toast and a cup of tea, then go to bed. Get up at 8, eat breakfast, and get to the test rested and on time. On the test, if I get stuck I'll skip that problem and go on to the end, then go back to the hard one if I have time.*

Emotional coping: *When I feel panicky and my hands start shaking, I'll close my eyes and just notice what I can hear and feel in this moment, focusing on what is going on around me here and now. If my mind goes blank I will sit back and do some deep breathing.*

Cognitive coping: *When I start thinking about failing and letting my mom and dad down, I'll use my mantra: "I know how to do this. I can take it one step at a time."*

Interpersonal coping: *Charles has agreed to check over the practice test I did last night, and my roommate says she will make sure I get to bed on time and will have breakfast with me.*

Susanna had to skip a couple of problems and go back to them after completing the rest. She completed all but one of the problems, got most of them correct, and passed with a B-minus.

One Exception

This chapter has shown you how to expand your thinking about your ability to cope, reminding you that even if the worst-case scenario comes to pass, there are things you can do to cope with life's challenges. However, there is one time when it is *not* helpful to use your coping skills: right before or during an exposure exercise. In those situations, the goal is to actually experience the habitual thoughts and feel the anxiety that they inspire, so using coping mechanisms then would lessen the therapeutic effectiveness of the exercise.

The next chapter teaches a powerful technique for dealing with fear in the moment.

CHAPTER 8

Reducing Worry with Defusion

When you are faced with a threat in life, it's natural to start predicting outcomes: what's going to happen in the next few minutes, tomorrow, next week, or next year? When the doctor tells you that your blood pressure is too high, your mind leaps to the future and you see yourself having to eat a very boring diet, gobble pills, struggle to get some kind of exercise, finally keeling over at an early age from a heart attack or stroke. Or you get a bad grade on a test and immediately you can see yourself flunking out, stuck in some menial job with no prospects, impoverished and alone.

Sometimes your worry about the future also includes rumination about the past. You dwell on how you might have brought high blood pressure on yourself with bad habits. You regret all the nights you stayed up late partying with your friends instead of studying.

A little of this is a good thing. Predicting outcomes, planning for the future, and learning from past mistakes are natural and beneficial. They are survival skills that help keep our species alive. But too much of this is a bad thing. When you think too long and too hard about all the things that can go wrong, you're not just planning for the future, you're worrying. When you ruminate obsessively on past mistakes and misfortunes, you're not learning from the past, you're just worrying about it.

In this chapter you will learn to respond to worry thoughts with a technique called *cognitive defusion*. The technique was developed by Steve Hayes, cofounder of acceptance and commitment therapy (Hayes and Wilson, 2003). Hayes realized that anxious people become "fused" with their fearful thoughts, *being* their thoughts instead of *having* their thoughts. He created a series of exercises designed to "defuse," or distance yourself from your thoughts by observing and labeling them.

Cognitive defusion is similar to some Buddhist meditation practices in which you observe your thoughts, label them, and then let them go. Where Buddhism is a spiritual practice in search of serenity and detachment from material desire, defusion is a psychological technique designed to reduce worry by creating distance between you and your fearful thoughts.

How Worry Drives Anxiety

In chapter 3 you assessed your anxiety in terms of what you are afraid will happen in the worst-case scenario, if everything you're afraid of were to come true in the most horrific way. If you habitually imagine catastrophic outcomes, it makes anxiety worse because your mind does not make a clear distinction between imagined events and real events. Both can trigger the same alarm response. Thinking intensely about spider bites, high buildings, or a disapproving boss can make your heart rate and breathing speed up just as much as seeing a real spider, going up in a glass elevator, or being criticized by your boss.

For example, Pam was afraid of getting into a head-on collision when she was driving. Hours before she had to drive somewhere she would review the route and think about all the undivided highways and left turns. She visualized a drunk driver coming the other way and suddenly veering into her lane. She imagined some distracted teenager not seeing her turn signal and plowing into her car at a busy intersection. She imagined the air bag exploding in her face, the sound of squealing tires and crunching metal, the smell of smoke and blood. By the time Pam got into her car, she was nervous and shaky because she had already been in a dozen accidents in her mind.

Visualization Exercise

Do this when you are alone and can sit quietly and comfortably, without interruption.

1. Recall the exercise in chapter 3 where you constructed an exposure hierarchy. Pick one of the situations, objects, people, or events that you rated as producing significant anxiety. Jot it down here, describing it in a few short words:

   _____

2. Circle a number below to rate how much anxiety you feel right now, just remembering the situation, object, person, or event.

   Mild anxiety   Moderate anxiety   Extreme anxiety

   1   2   3   4   5   6   7   8   9   10

3. Now get comfortable, close your eyes, and imagine that you are encountering the situation in real life. Visualize what and whom you see, the surroundings, the objects, and the action. Hear the sounds of people talking, traffic, whatever is making noise. Feel the warmth of the sun or the coolness of the breeze and the texture of things you touch. Make the scene vivid and real by using all your senses.

    As the encounter unfolds, imagine that the very worst outcome happens. Indulge your tendency to worry and ruminate and dwell on every catastrophic detail. Really wallow in the scary details and let yourself have a giant worry-fest.

4. Open your eyes and circle a number below to rate how much anxiety you feel now, after intensely worrying about the situation, object, person, or event.

Mild anxiety				Moderate anxiety				Extreme anxiety		
1	2	3	4	5	6	7	8	9	10	

What was your experience of this exercise? If you are like most people, the worrying will have increased your feelings anxiety. This is a small example of how your fear level is elevated and maintained at a high level by chronic worrying.

Learning to Observe Your Thoughts

When you worry, your thoughts follow one after another in a long sequence, each one connected to the one before and the one after in a seemingly unbreakable and inevitable chain of scary logic. One fear reminds you of another, and that brings up a third, and so on and so on.

One way to slow down this chaining and begin to separate the links is by observing your thoughts. Instead of just having a chain of thoughts, you take one tiny step backward and *watch yourself* having a chain of thoughts. It seems like a small distinction, but it makes a world of difference.

When you observe your thoughts instead of just having them, you create a little space, a separation that lessens the emotional impact of each thought. Try it for yourself in these two exercises.

News Crawl Exercise

1. Sit or lie comfortably in a quiet place where you won't be disturbed.

2. Close your eyes and relax by breathing slowly and deeply.

3. Imagine that your consciousness is a TV screen on which you see and hear everything that is going on. Since your eyes are closed right now and you are in a quiet space, the soundtrack is quiet and the screen is blank.

4. Visualize your thoughts as a "news crawl" at the bottom of the screen. Whatever you're thinking appears as moving captions, printed words at the bottom of the screen that appear on the right and move about as fast as you can read them to the left-hand side and disappear.

5. Just lie there and watch and read your thoughts, seeing them as news reports that randomly come up.

6. If your thoughts come too fast to put into complete sentences, just use single words or phrases as shorthand.

7. The news crawl might stall or blank out or repeat the same thought over and over. That's okay. Don't worry about it. Just wait patiently and see what happens.

8. For about five minutes, keep watching the news crawl of your thoughts until you see how they chain together, one thing connecting to another and another.

When Joan tried this exercise she stretched out on the couch late one afternoon and saw this news crawl: *Okay, this is weird … just watching words stream … how can this work? How long do I have to do this? Should be shopping … need bread and milk … Tom's dinner … he'll be late … really working? With somebody else … That blonde … Doesn't care … it's not fair … got to be careful … Don't say anything … be extra nice … no use anyway … he'll leave me …*

How was the exercise for you? Did you notice that the thoughts never really stop? Even if what you're thinking is *I'm not having any thoughts*, or *Maybe I'm doing this wrong*, those are thoughts.

If you had trouble with the news crawl stopping or blanking out, it might be that you think more in visual images than in words. The next exercise is probably better for you. If the same thought kept repeating, that's an indication of a particularly stubborn or "sticky" thought that is very central to your anxious feelings.

The experience of watching your thoughts as printed words at the bottom of a screen helps you see them more clearly, slow them down, and achieve some distance between you and your thoughts. It's a key experience of *having* thoughts instead of *being* your thoughts.

White Room Exercise

Some people experience their thoughts as vivid mental images rather than words. If you had trouble watching your thoughts as a news crawl of words, you might like this exercise better. It allows you to observe whatever visual imagery presents itself as part of a scary thought, and then label it with words. The basic idea is simple: see a thought, label it, and let it go.

1. In a quiet place where you won't be disturbed for a few minutes, sit or lie down comfortably. Relax a little by breathing slowly and deeply for several breaths.

2. Imagine that you are in a white room that is completely empty, with no furniture or decorations. You can position yourself in one of the corners, against a wall, up high by the ceiling, or near the floor—wherever feels right to you.

3. Visualize two open doorways, one on the right and one on the left. The doors are open into darkness. You can't see whatever is on the other side of the doorways.

4. Imagine that your thoughts enter the white room from the left doorway, pass in front of you, and exit through the right doorway. Your thoughts can take many forms: words, colors, sounds, images. You can represent your thoughts as animals or people or things. You might see a tough-looking thug, a nervous bunny, an orange pyramid, or just a vague cloud drifting by.

5. Some thoughts might move more slowly than others and want to stick around. Just let them move out the door. They might show up again, but keep them moving through the room and out the door. Don't worry if the same thoughts keep showing up.

6. As each thought appears, give it a label: "there's an anxious thought," or "there's a *what-if* thought," or "there's a catastrophic thought." As the thoughts walk or crawl or drift or drag themselves through the room, identify each one as a type. Don't analyze your thoughts at length; just come up with a short description.

7. Keep this up for five or ten minutes. Then remind yourself of your actual surroundings and open your eyes.

How was this exercise for you? Was it difficult to let some thoughts leave the room? Did some thoughts circle back and transit the room again and again? Were some thoughts harder to classify and label than others? Did you have the same kind of thought over and over? Or did you experience a variety of thoughts?

When Roberto did the White Room Exercise, he saw many of his thoughts in the form of people: he saw a homeless woman pushing a shopping cart and labeled it "a what-if thought about losing my job." He saw one thought as a stern police officer and labeled it "guilty." A crying little kid went through the room and Roberto labeled that thought "catastrophe thought."

Letting Go

Once you have some facility in observing your thoughts, your next task is to practice letting your thoughts go. The three exercises in this section draw on meditation techniques for letting distracting thoughts go and returning to focus on the present moment.

Present Moment Walk

1. Take your mind for a walk. Go for an actual walk outdoors.

2. Focus your attention on the things you are seeing, hearing, and feeling: the ground beneath your feet, the buildings and trees and people, the weather, the sounds you hear.

3. Inevitably you will be distracted by random thoughts. They may be anxiety thoughts or thoughts about anything. Notice each thought, then let it go and return your attention to the present moment—what you see, hear, and feel.

4. Continue this process for ten or fifteen minutes, noticing and letting go of distracting thoughts, continually returning your attention to the here and now. The goal of this exercise is not to keep your attention fixed on the walk, but to repeatedly have the experience of being distracted by your thoughts, noticing that you are distracted, and returning your attention to your surroundings.

How did you do? Were you surprised by how many thoughts came up? It is remarkably difficult to concentrate on the here and now. When Darcy took her Present Moment Walk, she found herself thinking about an upcoming dinner party, then returned her attention to the bike trail she was walking on. But thoughts of the dinner kept intruding: whether everybody liked Brussels sprouts, should she invite Jack's coworker, did she have enough plates that matched, and so on. At one point, she was so distracted that a man on a recumbent bike almost mowed her down.

Breath Counting

1. Sit or lie down in a comfortable spot where you won't be disturbed.

2. Focus your mind on your breathing—taking a slow, deep breath, holding it for a second, and then letting it out in a gradual exhale.

3. Count your breaths. You can count one on the first inhale, two on the exhale, three on the next inhale, and so on. Or just count complete breaths—whatever feels right to you.

4. Very soon a thought will intrude. Again, it can be a fearful thought or not, but for sure it will take your attention away from counting your breaths.

5. When a thought comes up, notice it, then let it go and return to counting your breaths.

6. If the thought makes you lose count, start over at one.

7. Keep this up for five to ten minutes, counting breaths, noticing any distracting thoughts, letting them go, and returning to breath counting.

This is a simple but profound experience, basic to several meditation traditions. How did you do? Did you get so distracted that you lost count? Did you get better at noticing the thoughts more quickly, or did the more interesting thoughts carry you away into an extended reverie? There's no wrong way to do this exercise, since the goal is to notice how often your mind wanders away from the task at hand, and how you notice the distractions and return your focus to the here and now.

Leaves on a Stream

1. Lie or sit down comfortably in a spot where you will not be disturbed. Relax by breathing slowly and deeply.

2. Imagine that you are on the edge of a slow-moving stream, on a quiet day in fall. See the red and orange and brown leaves on the shore. Sometimes a leaf falls into the steam and floats away.

3. When you have a thought, place it on one of the floating leaves and let it drift out of sight. Return to enjoying the streamside until the next distracting thought arises. Place this thought on a leaf as well and let it float away downstream.

4. You can sum up your thoughts in a word or phrase, or use little images that you place on the leaves.

5. Don't try to make the stream move faster or slower, and don't change what you put on the leaves. Just let them float away.

6. For five or six minutes, as each thought comes up, put it on a leaf and let it float away.

7. Don't be surprised or worried if your stream won't flow or you get stuck with one thought on a leaf that doesn't want to go away. The whole scene might even disappear for a while. That's all right. Just recreate the scene and carry on as best you can.

8. Open your eyes and record your experience: whether your stream wouldn't flow, or the scene disappeared for a while, or whatever happened:

_____

_____

If you could not get a clear image of the scene, describe what you were thinking about while attempting the exercise:

_____

_____

Did you enjoy the stream imagery and letting your thoughts float away on the leaves? This exercise can show how persistent and "sticky" some thoughts are, and that you can eventually let them go. If you had trouble getting your stream to flow or got stuck on leaf, that's cognitive *fusion*. When your stream was flowing freely and you could let leaves go, that's cognitive *defusion*.

Some people prefer to do this exercise with different kinds of scenes: attaching thoughts to helium balloons and releasing them to disappear into the sky; or imaging that they are in their car at a railroad crossing, watching boxcar after boxcar carry their thoughts away.

Carl liked to do this exercise using the boxcars. He visualized himself in his pickup truck, watching the train cars go by with his thoughts spray painted on them like graffiti: *father-in-law … graduation … stupid exercise … need a tune up … nervous …* When Carl thought of specific people he sometimes saw them as photographic posters pasted on the boxcars, or as actual human figures clinging to the ladders and couplings. Once he put a poster of his wife on a boxcar and the train stopped moving and he couldn't get it to start up again for quite a while.

Distancing

When you have a "sticky" recurring thought that often causes you anxiety, consider these four questions:

1. **How old is this?** When can you remember first having this thought? Was it years ago, when you were a little kid? Does it date back to your school days? Did it start when you began dating? When you started working for a living? Recalling the history of this thought will remind you that it is just a thought. You have survived all this time while having this thought frequently, and you are still alive, still carrying on from day to day. Juliana often thought, *He's out of my league*, whenever she was introduced to a new guy. The thought went back to grade school, when she never felt like one of the cool kids, and always considered herself the last to be chosen, the least interesting, the bottom of the social barrel.

2. **What's its purpose?** Think about why your mind keeps throwing up this thought. What is it in service of? Is your mind trying to warn you of danger, protect you from risk, help you avoid rejection or failure? For Juliana, the thought *He's out of my league* was serving to keep her safe from the pain of rejection. If she never tried to fit in and make friends or find a boyfriend, she would never be excluded or dumped.

3. **Has it worked?** How well has this habitual fearful thought worked out for you? Have you felt safe, protected, secure, and happy? Evaluating the success of your anxious thought will highlight the consequences of *being* your thought instead of *having* your thought. Fear of being mugged might keep you "safe" at home, but over time you become isolated and lonely, while your friends and loved ones carry on with fuller lives without you. For Juliana, the result of thinking *He's out of my league* was years of

loneliness. She avoided social gatherings and didn't even like to make phone calls to the few friends she had. By trying to avoid possible rejection, she cut herself off from any kind of acceptance and love. She ended up rejecting herself before anyone else could reject her.

4. **Can I tolerate it?** This is the payoff question. By answering the first three questions, you have distanced yourself from your habitual thought, defusing yourself from your mind so that you can *have* the thought without *being* the thought. Ask yourself now if you are willing to take your thought with you, while you pursue what you really want in life. Complete this statement in your own words:

I can take this thought with me and still:

_____

_____

Juliana completed her distancing exercise like this:

I can take this thought with me and still:

Talk to men I meet, accept invitations, and initiate phone calls.

Defusion in Everyday Life

As you go about your day-to-day existence, the same old thoughts will continue to come up:

I might run someone over.

They don't like me.

What if get so nervous I throw up?

That looks so germy.

I can't stand it.

I'll fall.

Strangers! Careful!

When you have your fearful thoughts again, remember the defusion skills you have mastered in this chapter. You can imagine that the thoughts are merely a news crawl at the bottom of your screen, not the main program you are intent on watching. You can say to yourself, *There's that thought again, passing through the white room of my mind*, and continue on your way. You can distance yourself from your thought by saying to your mind, *Thank you, mind, for that thought.*

When a thought keeps intruding, you can refocus your attention on your surroundings, seeing and hearing what is around you in the here and now, like you did in the "Present Moment Walk." Or you can focus your attention on your breathing and count two or three breaths to calm and distract yourself from the thought.

You can also label thoughts as they come up: *Oh, there's another stranger/danger thought … there's a catastrophic prediction again … I'm magnifying risk now.* Imagine letting these labeled thoughts float away like leaves in a stream, balloons in the air, or boxcars on a train track.

One Exception

There is one time when it is *not* helpful to use your defusion skills: right before or during an exposure exercise. In those situations, the goal is to actually experience the habitual thoughts and feel the anxiety that they inspire, so using defusion then would lessen the therapeutic effectiveness of the exercise.

The next chapter presents a new auxiliary skill in your anxiety arsenal: correcting your anxiety lens.

CHAPTER 9

Correcting Your Anxiety Lens

Anxiety is like a distorting lens through which you view the world. Your anxiety lens filters out rays of hope, blocks your view of possible good outcomes, blurs anything positive, brings the negative into sharp focus, and magnifies any kind of threat in your life.

You are probably reading this chapter because in chapter 2 you identified *misappraisal* as one of the problems that significantly contributes to your anxiety. Misappraisal is the inaccurate or distorted assessment of danger or threat. When you consistently overestimate the level of threat you are facing, you set yourself up for chronic anxiety.

All misappraisals of threat arise from three negative thinking patterns, or habits of perception that distort reality. The three negative thinking patterns that comprise the anxiety lens are:

1. Negative Predictions

2. Negative Focus

3. Problem Magnification

In this chapter you will determine which of these negative thinking patterns you use most often and practice exercises that will help you correct your anxiety lens, more accurately assess threats, and reduce your anxiety.

Assessing Your Thinking Patterns

The first step in correcting your anxiety lens is to practice identifying the three negative thinking patterns. In the first exercise you will analyze typical anxiety thoughts and categorize them. In the second exercise you will do the same, using your own anxiety thoughts from a Thought Log that you keep for a week.

Your mind does its best to prepare you for possible danger, assess your ability to cope, and keep you safe. It's part of your human survival instinct. But sometimes the anxiety your mind creates is more of a problem than the threats it seeks to avoid. The exercises in this section will allow you to take a step back from your thoughts, to notice how your mind's natural survival instinct can go too far, and to see how your anxiety thoughts go beyond protecting you and instead make you feel scared and unable to cope. Take your time doing these exercises and don't skimp on them. They will lay down a solid foundation of analytical skill that will serve you well in the rest of the chapter and the rest of your life.

Recognizing Negative Thinking Patterns

This exercise will give you practice in discriminating among negative predictions, negative focus, and problem magnification. To get you started, here are some examples of the three types of negative thinking:

Negative predictions:

I'm going to lose my job.

This backache is going to get worse and require surgery.

If I'm late with the rent we'll be evicted.

He's going to dump me.

Negative focus:

Her class is so boring.

My life is just one problem after another.

Nobody ever gives me a break.

I can't stand how insensitive he is.

Problem magnification:

The stress is killing me.

It's impossible.

I'll never get there on time.

This wedding is a total disaster.

Now that you have some idea of the differences among the three negative thought patterns, categorize the anxiety thoughts below as:

    A. Negative predictions

    B. Negative focus

    C. Problem magnification

1.   __A__ *Example: I'm going to flunk out.*

2.   _____ *The whole house is falling apart.*

3.   _____ *I'm never going to get out of this town.*

4.   _____ *She never calls, and when she does, she hangs up after five minutes.*

5.   _____ *He's nothing but trouble.*

6.   _____ *My daughter is so late, I know she's been in an accident.*

7.   _____ *This lecture is boring.*

8.   _____ *Every time I come here it's so frustrating.*

9.   _____ *I'll probably die alone.*

10.   _____ *The soup was bland; the dinner was just awful.*

Answer key: 2. C, 3. A, 4. B, 5. C, 6. A, 7. B, 8. C, 9. A, 10 B.

How did you do? Don't worry if you got some wrong answers. It is not easy to make these subtle distinctions among the three types of negative thinking that lead to anxiety. They tend to overlap and blend into each other, since all anxiety is to some degree concerned with predicting the future, highlighting the negative, and magnifying problems. And short statements like these are open to subjective interpretation. You will probably find the next exercise easier, when you are dealing with your own anxiety thoughts, expressed in your own words, in situations where you know the full details.

Thought Log

For the next week, keep a Thought Log. Whenever you feel anxious, jot down a few words to sum up what you are thinking. Then note whether the thought is primarily negative prediction, negative focus, or problem magnification.

   Make several copies of this worksheet so you'll have enough for the week. (A downloadable version of this worksheet is available at http://www.newharbinger.com/34749.)

Thought Log

Thought	Negative prediction	Negative focus	Problem magnification

After a week, look back at your log and notice which type of negative thinking pattern most often creates your anxiety. Take some time to consider how your habits of thought have contributed to painful anxiety over the course of your life.

The exercises that follow are organized according to which of the three negative thinking patterns they most directly target. You should read over all of them to familiarize yourself with the various methods of correcting your anxiety lens. Then go back and really get to work on the exercises that are most appropriate for your particular style of misappraisal.

Negative Prediction Exercises

This whole chapter is designed to increase your cognitive flexibility. Cognitive flexibility means that you are able to come up with several explanations or interpretations for any event or situation. This section teaches three ways to handle negative predictions flexibly: by calculating the "Validity Quotient," by keeping a Predictions Log, and by exploring the purpose of your predictions.

Calculating the Validity Quotient

This exercise will give you a concrete number to score how accurately your negative predictions forecast the future. It targets a single negative prediction, going back five years in your life to count how many times the prediction has come true.

Pick a negative prediction that you often find yourself making. It can be something you worry about happening to your kids; in your primary relationship; or in your finances, health, job, or school situation. Sum up the negative prediction in a few words and write it here:

_____

In the last five years, how many times have you made this prediction?
Estimate the number of times and write it here: _____

How many times in the last five years has this prediction come true?
Count up the number of times and write it here: _____

Divide the second number by the first number and write the result here:

Validity Quotient   _____

This calculation gives you the Validity Quotient, the exact odds of your negative prediction coming true. If you are like most anxious people, this number will be a very small fraction or decimal number—way less than 1. Here is an example of how Conrad determined the Validity Quotient of his worries about his teenage son's driving:

Donny's so reckless, I worry he's going to crash the car and hurt himself.

In the last five years, how many times have you made this prediction?
Estimate the number of times and write it here: 250

How many times in the last five years has this prediction come true? Count up the number of times and write it here: 1

Divide the second number by the first number and write the result here:

Validity Quotient   0.004

In the past five years, Conrad's son Donny had had one small fender bender that gave him a sore neck for a couple of days. Conrad realized that he had spent hours and hours worrying about Donny getting in an accident, when in fact the likelihood, the Validity Quotient of that negative prediction, was very small.

Keeping a Predictions Log

In the previous exercise, you worked on past predictions. In this exercise you will keep track of your negative predictions as they occur, jotting them down in the Predictions Log that follows. From time to time you will review what you have written and see which predictions have come true.

Over the next week or two, carry a copy of the log with you. Every time you catch yourself worrying about the future, write down a brief summary of the negative predictions you are making in your mind. (A downloadable version of this contract is available at http://www .newharbinger.com/34749.)

Predictions Log

Predictions (What terrible thing will happen and when)	What actually occurred

When the predicted time of each terrible thing arrives, get out your Predictions Log and note what actually occurred. How many of your predictions came true? Of those that did come true, if any, how many were as terrible as you thought they would be?

When Jenny did this exercise, she was approaching finals week at the junior college where she was taking nursing classes. She wrote six different predictions about her school work: that she would flunk Anatomy, that she'd get a bad grade in Statistics, that her advisor would make her switch to a lab tech program, and so on. Of all six catastrophic predictions, only one actually occurred. She got a C-minus in Statistics, which didn't look very good on her record, but she passed. Keeping her Predictions Log helped Jenny see that her negative predictions were just thoughts, not sure things. She felt a little less anxious about her classes, more confident about her career choice, and calmer when she went to see her advisor to plan the next semester.

Questioning the Purpose of Predictions

This exercise is simple. When you catch yourself making negative predictions about the future, ask yourself these two questions:

1. **What is the purpose of this prediction?**

2. **Is this prediction accomplishing its purpose?**

Every activity has a purpose, including the mental activity of thinking about the future and making predictions. You will find that the purpose of negative predictions is almost always the same: to reduce uncertainty, to prepare you for bad things that might happen, and to somehow keep you safe. And you will find that the answer to question number 2 is almost always the same: Your predictions make you feel more anxious and threatened, not less. Dwelling on catastrophic visions of the future does not make you feel more secure, does not make you feel more prepared, and does not make you feel safe.

When you notice that you are worrying and making negative predictions, ask yourself these two questions and let the answers serve as a reminder that your anxious thoughts are not accomplishing anything. This will help you notice your thoughts, take them less seriously, and let them go more easily.

Negative Focus Exercises

Your anxiety lens focuses your awareness on the negative aspects of any situation, exaggerating dangers, ramping up your feelings of fear, and blinding you to the positive factors in the situation. The first two exercises in this section will help you expand your focus, and the third will analyze the purpose of negative focus.

Big Picture Awareness

Viewing your life constantly through the lens of anxiety can be like watching a horror or action movie shot entirely in close-up. Everything is huge, fast, and scary. It's confusing and claustrophobic. You never see a wide shot in which you can relax, get your bearings, clearly identify everything that is going on, and understand a scene from a comfortable distance.

When you focus consistently on the negative it's like listening to music and hearing only the dissonant, sour notes. Whether you are thinking about your job, an upcoming trip or move, your relationship, your health, or where you live, you zero in on the negative details that turn everything dark and frightening.

The way to modify this cognitive habit is to regularly step back and look at the big picture. After you have said or thought something negative about a situation, find at least two things that are positive about it. Make this a rule—that for each negative appraisal you make of a situation, experience, or person, you will come up with two positive aspects.

Here is a list of possible considerations that will help you find the positive in a situation that at first appears only negative. Keep a copy of these on an index card and carry it with you in your purse or pocket.

- Physical pleasure or comfort

- Pleasant emotions

- Calm, peace, rest, relaxation

- Feelings of accomplishment, completion, satisfaction

- The opportunity to learn something new

- Closeness, connection to someone

- Being loved or appreciated

- Finding value or meaning

- The chance to give or be of service

When you find that you are focusing on the negative, take a look at the ideas on your index card. Balance your perspective by identifying two positive aspects of what you are thinking about.

It's not wrong or stupid to make negative evaluations, and they might even be true. But it's one-sided. There are always some positive aspects to every situation, and ignoring them leads to chronic anxiety.

For example, Joyce was looking for a better job. She hated making calls on the phone to follow up on resumes she had emailed. All she could see when she contemplated calling a prospective employer was that she was very vulnerable, that she was opening herself up for rejection. She consulted her index card of possible positives and reminded herself that the calls were a chance to learn valuable information about each company, and that she would feel a sense of accomplishment by making the calls.

Remember that nearly all experiences are a blend of the pleasant and the unpleasant, the positive and the negative. Widening your focus to include the big picture will make your habitual thinking patterns more flexible and less likely to lead straight to anxiety.

Seeing Both Sides of the Coin

Most painful experiences have a flip side—some beneficial lesson learned, insight gained, friendship deepened, or ability improved. This tendency for a bad experience to include an opposite, compensatory good experience is the basis for clichés like "What doesn't kill you makes you stronger" and "Every cloud has a silver lining."

Your anxiety lens prevents you from easily seeing the other side of the coin, but it's there. The dreaded airplane flight does eventually deliver you to some place you want or need to go. The terrifying speech or interview can lead to acclaim or a better job. The walk past the neighbor's barking dogs gives you a shorter route home and the satisfaction of overcoming fear.

As with the previous Big Picture Awareness exercise, the positive aspects of painful situations tend to lie in certain categories:

- Getting in touch with new determination or strength

- Learning something new

- Achieving greater acceptance

- Letting go of attachments to certain outcomes

- Appreciating others' struggles

- Glimpsing new or hidden parts of yourself

- Receiving unexpected support and love from others

- Increasing confidence in your ability to cope

- Affirming your values and what is most important to you

Practice seeing both sides of the coin by filling out the worksheet below with three negative experiences you have had, and the possible positive sides of those experiences.

Both Sides Worksheet

Negative experience	Positive side of the coin

John used this exercise to explore his experiences as a bookkeeper for a large nonprofit foundation. He had been anxious about making mistakes, getting fired, and being unemployed. Going to work seemed like a purely stressful and tense experience, but he thought long and hard about the positive side of the coin. He realized that he did enjoy and value the two colleagues with whom he ate lunch once a week. A positive evaluation from his supervising accountant—something that usually would make him think, *I fooled them for another year*—this time gave him a feeling of job satisfaction. And finally, he realized that he really did value the philanthropic programs that his organization financed. He felt that he was contributing something positive and doing something worthwhile by going to work every day.

Understanding the Purpose of Negative Focus

Every human behavior has a purpose, even thought. Negative focus tends to have one or more of these purposes:

- Discharging anxiety that has built up during stressful experiences

- Lowering expectations

- Avoiding disappointment

- Avoiding future stressful experiences

- Improving yourself by doing better or correcting errors or faults

Think about the negative thoughts that you tend to dwell on. Which of these purposes could your thoughts be trying to achieve? You might even come up with a purpose we haven't listed.

The key question is this: Are your negative thoughts achieving their purpose? Are they discharging anxiety, helping you avoid disappointment, or making you a better person? If they are, that's good. But since you are reading this book, chances are that your negative focus goes too far, goes beyond any reasonable purpose, and is just causing you distress.

Fact is, most people overdo negative focus and get no benefit from it. They feel more pain, not less. They cannot avoid all future stressful situations. Their anxious thoughts make them feel less safe, not more.

When you find that you are focusing on the negative, ask yourself whether your thoughts are really serving any beneficial purpose. If they are not benefiting you, label those thoughts as unnecessary negative focus. Tell yourself, "There's one of my negative, anxiety-provoking thoughts again." Just labeling the thoughts will create distance and allow you to let them go. Of course, they will return, but when they do you will know how to question their purpose and let them go again. Eventually, these thoughts will become less potent and troubling.

Problem Magnification Exercises

When your anxiety lens magnifies problems, they become too huge to surmount. They dominate your mental landscape, fence you into a cage of anxiety, and prevent you from moving forward in your life. The exercises in this final section of the chapter will help you dial down the magnification factor, correct your anxiety lens, and view your problems as something closer to their actual size.

Problem Continuum

One way to judge size is by comparison to nearby objects. This exercise places your current problems on a continuum, or scale, of problems that range from huge to tiny. Read over the list of problems that follow and pick the largest, worst one. Rewrite it in the top blank space in the middle column. Then pick the next largest problem and rewrite that one in the second space in the middle column. Continue until you have ranked all the problems from biggest to smallest.

Then pick your own largest problem, the thing you worry about most. Write it down in one of the spaces on the right, picking a spot where it fits in the continuum of problems, across from a problem of about the same size, with a larger problem above it and a smaller problem below it. Do this with one or two other problems you worry about. (A downloadable version of this contract is available at http://www.newharbinger.com/34749.)

Problem Continuum Worksheet

Problems	Problem continuum	
	(Rank big to small)	Your problems
A terminal diagnosis	_____	_____
Death of a loved one	_____	_____
Loss of your job	_____	_____
House foreclosure	_____	_____
Divorce/breakup	_____	_____
Mild criticism from your boss	_____	_____
Mild disagreement with a friend	_____	_____
Loss of your wallet	_____	_____
A big auto repair bill	_____	_____
Car breakdown—need to be towed	_____	_____
Refrigerator needs replacing	_____	_____
Late for work	_____	_____

When Sherrie did this exercise, she found that visiting her sick mother-in-law, driving on the bridge, and going to the dentist, which all seemed enormous to her, barely made it halfway up the problem continuum. It put her problems in perspective and made her grateful that she still had her health and her husband and a job.

Just the Facts

If you forget your glasses in a restaurant, you can have a friend read the blurry words on the menu for you. This exercise works kind of the same way. Since you sometimes see the world through a distorting anxiety lens, you are going to imagine that your problems are being viewed and described for you, by someone else.

Do you have a level-headed friend whom nothing ever seems to bother? One of those practical, resilient, down-to-earth folks who seldom worries? The kind who stays calm in frantic situations and says things like, "Relax and don't sweat the small stuff"?

Imagine that kind of person describing your problems for you. Actually close your eyes, take a couple of deep breaths, and imagine that you can hear that person's voice, speaking in the first person (as you), talking about your situation and your fears. Listen to the voice of your friend using neutral, accurate, factual words to lay out your life.

In the space below, sum up what you hear in this imaginary description.

_____

_____

_____

_____

When George did this exercise, he imagined his second cousin Marjorie describing his relationship and living situation. George had just moved into a very expensive apartment with his new girlfriend, Carol, who made a lot more money than he did, came from a wealthy family, and had Champagne and caviar tastes. George's own mental summary of his situation went something like this:

I'm screwed. I'm way out of my league with Carol. I don't dare tell her I can't afford this place. I'm barely making it and she wants to have the place painted and buy a gazillion bucks' worth of furniture. As soon as she sees what a cheapskate loser I am, she's sure to dump me.

When George imagined Cousin Marjorie describing his situation, it sounded more factual, more confident, and a lot less dire:

I'm not sure Carol realizes I can't swing a full half of these expenses. I need to make it clear that if she wants this kind of lifestyle, she'll have to pay for more than half. If that bothers her, I'm better off knowing now, and so is she. Hopefully, our relationship is more important to her than furniture, but if not, I guess I'm also better off knowing that now.

The Day in History

This exercise is simplicity itself. It's based on the truisms that things change, time marches on, and nothing lasts forever. When you are obsessing about one of your problems, ask yourself this simple question: How long will I remember this problem and be worried about it? (Choose one.)

__ 2 days

__ 1–2 weeks

__ 1 month

__ 6 months

__ 1 year

__ 5 years

__ 10 years

__ Until I die

Clarice was worried about her upcoming wedding—the venue, the dress, the flowers, the registry, the guest list, the million details that kept her up at night and made her so tense she would snap at anyone who had the temerity to tell her to calm down and relax. It helped to ask herself, "How long will I remember this problem? Will I be insanely worried forever?" She realized that the day after the wedding her worry would plummet. By the time she experienced her first anniversary, giving birth to a child, or buying a house, she would have forgotten almost all the worries of the wedding. Clarice still worried about her wedding, but taking the long view once in a while kept things a bit more in perspective, and allowed her to be less of what her maid of honor called "Monster Bride."

One Exception

There is one time when you *should not* use the new techniques you've learned in this chapter: while you are doing the exposure exercises in the earlier chapters in this book. The whole point of exposure treatment is to fully experience the anxiety associated with specific situations, thoughts, or events. During those highly structured exercises, using the techniques in this chapter can actually make results take longer to achieve. So save your anxiety lens correction skills for those times when you are not actively working on specific fears. Use them when you catch yourself in garden-variety worrying, in a free-floating state of anxiety.

Correcting your anxiety lens is a long-term project. Continuing to do the exercises in this chapter will help you develop new habits of thought over time. It's like getting glasses for the first time. At first you forget to put them on in the morning, you leave them on your dining room table or in your car, or you reach for them and can't immediately recall where you left them. But eventually you develop the habits that keep your glasses within arm's reach. Likewise, repeated practice will keep your anxiety-reduction habits fresh. You'll remember to analyze your negative predictions, sweeten your negative focus, and cut your problem magnification down to actual size.

Turn to the next chapter to learn the last of the auxiliary skills for handling anxiety: distress tolerance.

CHAPTER 10

Distress Tolerance Skills

Distress tolerance is one of those rare psychological terms whose meaning is clear. It means the ability to experience negative stress without being overwhelmed by painful feelings. It is a skill that you can learn and improve upon, just as you might work on improving your tennis or bridge game. It is not an inborn characteristic like blue eyes that you either have or don't have.

Distress tolerance is a key skill taught in dialectical behavior therapy to handle situations that are impossible or very difficult to change, such as divorce, job loss, or health problems. Distress tolerance is an acquired resilience that helps you regulate the anxiety you feel in such challenging life experiences (Linehan, 1993).

In this chapter you will learn five ways to improve your distress tolerance skills: mindfulness, relaxation, self-soothing, positive distraction, and coping thoughts. These are all techniques that will help you reduce anxiety in stressful situations that you can't or shouldn't avoid.

There is one time when you should not use the distress tolerance techniques you learn in this chapter: when you are doing the exposure exercises you learned in the earlier chapters of the book. Since research has shown that exposure exercises work best and fastest when you fully experience the target emotion of anxiety, using distress tolerance techniques at the same time will just make exposure take longer.

Mindfulness

Mindfulness is a centuries-old practice that originated in Eastern religions. In Western psychology, mindfulness has become an important part of emotional awareness in all three of the universal treatments for emotional disorders: dialectical behavior therapy, cognitive behavioral therapy, and acceptance and commitment therapy.

There are three aspects of mindfulness: awareness, acceptance, and present-focus. First, you experience the world around you with all your senses while at the same time being aware of your internal sensations. Second, you observe without judgment, without being for or against what you perceive. Third, you confine your perceptions to the present moment, letting go of all thoughts of the past or future.

Mindfulness helps reduce anxiety by shifting your attention away from ruminating on the past or dreading the future. It also allows you to see that your anxiety is only a part of the present moment, and that anxious thoughts and feelings are transitory—arising, peaking, and declining over time.

Five Senses

This is a simple exercise you can do in two or three minutes, almost any time. Just pay attention to what each of your senses is telling you, taking the five senses in turn:

1. *Sight*: Spend about half a minute looking around and listing all the things you can see.

2. *Sound*: Then close your eyes and listen to whatever sounds you can hear.

3. *Smell*: What do you smell right now?

4. *Taste*: Are you aware of any particular tastes?

5. *Touch*: How warm or cold are you? Does anything itch or hurt? Where do you feel pressure or weight?

Distracting or judgmental thoughts will pop up: *This is silly*, or *There's that stupid dog barking again*. When that happens, let the thought go and return to cataloging your sensations. You'll be surprised how calming and centering this exercise can be.

Mindful Breathing

Breathing meditations have been used for thousands of years in many cultures. When you pay attention to your breathing, you automatically take attention away from your anxious thoughts. Mindful breathing has three components: attending to your breath, labeling each breath, and letting go of distracting thoughts.

1. Sit in a comfortable chair or lie down on your back with your arms and legs uncrossed. Close your eyes and notice your breath. You can focus on your

diaphragm area at the bottom of your rib cage that rises and falls when you breathe. Or you can concentrate on the path of the air from your nose to your throat and down into your chest. Become conscious of the subtle changes in the temperature of the moving air, the feelings of pressure and release, and the sounds of your breathing.

2. Label your breathing by saying "in" to yourself as you inhale and "out" as you exhale. Or you might count your breaths, saying "one" to yourself on the first exhalation, then "two" on the next exhalation, and so on. Most teachers suggest starting over after "four." Experiment with different labeling methods until you settle on the one you like best.

3. Notice and let go of each thought that comes up. Don't be discouraged if you experience a steady stream of distracting thoughts. That's natural and to be expected. As soon as you notice that your attention has shifted away from your breathing, say to yourself, "thought," and return your focus to your breathing. Many meditation experts say that the essence and most valuable part of meditation is this shift from distraction back to your intended focus.

Mindful breathing works best if you do it two or three times daily. Start with two-minute sessions. After a few days, increase to three minutes for a few more days, then go to four or five minutes.

Mindfulness of Emotions

Once you have experienced mindful breathing for a while, you can go on to mindfulness of emotions, a systematic way of observing the natural ebb and flow of painful feelings without being swept away by them. This technique is particularly helpful when you are starting to feel anxious about something, especially if you are tempted to avoid the feeling. Trying to avoid anxiety makes it stronger and more enduring. Practicing mindfulness of anxiety makes it weaker and briefer.

The secret to this skill is to allow the feelings of fear and nervousness to exist. Don't try to block or stifle them. Every emotion is like a wave in that it starts small, grows to a crest, and then declines. If you observe this happening, without amplifying the feeling, analyzing it, or judging yourself, then you will get a clear picture of the temporary nature of emotions.

1. When you're feeling a painful emotion and it is possible to get some privacy, get comfortable and close your eyes. Focus on your feeling and give it a name: *fear*,

nervousness, resentment, guilt, sadness, and so on. Ask yourself how strong the feeling is, and whether there is just one feeling or several mixed together.

2. Pause and attend to your breathing for a few breaths, making it slow and regular, paying attention to the air flowing into your nose and down your windpipe, filling your trunk, and flowing out again.

3. When thoughts come up, label them: *judgment, planning for the future, memory,* and so on. Then return to observing your breath and your inner emotional state.

4. Expand your awareness. Notice any physical sensations in your body. Listen for sounds around you. Imagine space extending around you wider and wider, until you are aware of your neighborhood, your continent, the planet, the solar system, the universe of stars and planets.

5. Stay with this exercise, cycling from your feelings to your breath to the universe, until the original feeling subsides, until it changes into a different feeling, or until you feel you have done enough for now.

Watching your emotions like this allows you to see them for what they are: feelings that come and go while you continue to live in the full context of your existence. It's like feelings are weather and you are the sky. Weather constantly changes, but the sky remains the sky. Sometimes the weather can get very violent and scary, but it never destroys the sky. The sky persists no matter how dark the clouds, and eventually the sun always comes out again.

Carol, a bookkeeper for a casino in Nevada, was terrified of being assaulted when she had to drive downtown or to the store after dark. When she had to drive after dark, she used mindfulness to calm herself before starting the car. When she parked at the store or on a downtown street, she would take a minute to watch her emotions and sense impressions before getting out of the car. While she was shopping or dining, she would label her intrusive fearful thoughts: *planning … worrying … living in the future.*

Relaxation

Many different cultures and traditions use attention to your breathing as a way to relax.

Diaphragmatic Breathing

When you're feeling anxious, your body tenses and your breathing becomes faster and more shallow. By consciously slowing your breathing and drawing air deep into your lungs with your diaphragm, you send your body a strong message that everything is okay and it can relax. Your diaphragm is the wide, strong sheet of muscle at the bottom of your rib cage. It moves down and out to fully inflate your lungs and moves up to push air out of your lungs. The instructions for diaphragmatic breathing are simple.

1. Find a quiet place where you won't be bothered for about five minutes. Lie down on your back with your arms and legs uncrossed. Or sit up straight in an upright chair.

2. Put your hand on your stomach just below your rib cage and breathe in slowly through your nose. Feel how the inhalation pushes your hand out as you breathe deeply into your belly.

3. Exhale fully through your mouth and feel how your stomach moves inward as your diaphragm moves in and up.

4. Continue to breathe in through your nose and out through your mouth, observing how your hand moves out and in. Notice how your body feels more and more relaxed as you breathe this way.

5. Your mind will wander over the next five minutes. When it does, return your awareness to your breath and your diaphragm.

Practicing diaphragmatic breathing two or three times a day will go a long way toward increasing your distress tolerance.

Cue-Controlled Relaxation

When you have become familiar with the relaxing feeling of your mindfulness or breathing exercises, you can use cue-controlled relaxation to very quickly lower your feelings of tension or anxiety. To prepare, choose a "cue word" that you will use to remind yourself of what relaxation feels like. It can be *calm … relax … easy* or any other word that appeals to you.

Close your eyes for a moment and scan your body for tension. Notice wherever your muscles are holding tension. Then say your cue word to yourself and let your whole body relax.

Denny's cue word was *serenity*. He pictured the word carved in flowing script on a hardwood log, deep in the forest. When he was feeling nervous about entering a meeting at work or making a confrontational phone call, he would close his eyes, take a deep diaphragmatic breath, and say "serenity" to himself, imagining that he was seeing the word carved into the log, surrounded by the peaceful woods. It helped a great deal to remind him of his relaxation skills and allowed him to let go of tension quickly.

Self-Soothing

Any activity, experience, or pastime that you enjoy or that relaxes you can qualify as self-soothing. It can be listening to music, playing an instrument, reading, taking a walk, knitting, painting a picture, or some other kind of craft or hobby. (Dangerous or destructive habits such as drinking, taking drugs, or driving recklessly are not appropriate.) Self-soothing is one of the key distress tolerance skills taught in dialectical behavior therapy (Linehan, 1993).

Take the time to soothe yourself by feeding your five senses. Watch a sunset; listen to a song; taste and smell good food; wear soft, comfortable clothes.

Sight

Since sight is perhaps your most important connection with the outside world, what you look at can have profound effects on tension and relaxation. Look over this list of pleasures involving sight, check off those you want to try, and add any other items you can think of:

☐ Go to a favorite spot and just look at water or mountains or art in a gallery.

☐ Carry a favorite photo in your wallet or purse that you can pull out and look at whenever you want.

☐ Put up pictures on your walls at home and at work.

☐ Get picture books from the library of whatever you like to look at.

☐ Make a drawing or a collage of images that please you.

☐ Other: _____

☐ Other: _____

☐ Other: _____

Hearing

What you hear has a huge effect on how you feel. Have you ever watched a movie with the sound muted? It's amazing how much the emotional impact of a scene is created by the music and other sounds. Taking the time to add pleasant sounds to your environment can lower your stress level in a big way. Try some of these suggestions, or add favorites of your own:

☐ Listen to an audiobook. Most libraries have a selection. You don't even have to follow the storyline closely. Just hearing a human voice in the background can be soothing.

☐ Listen to the kind of music you like best. Pop, classical, jazz, new age, world—it doesn't matter as long as you enjoy it.

☐ Use the TV or a fan as white noise to relax you. Turn the sound down low so that it is like a babbling brook, a soothing background mumble.

☐ Or actually listen to a white noise recording or machine. This can mask other distracting or annoying sounds such as traffic or noisy neighbors.

☐ Get a fountain that you like the sound of.

☐ Open the window so you can hear the birdsong and wind and other natural sounds. Or if your window doesn't offer that option, get a recording of nature sounds that you like.

☐ Other: _____

☐ Other: _____

☐ Other: _____

Taste

You have to eat and drink every day, so why not make meals and snacks an opportunity for self-soothing? On the other hand, if you are overweight because you already do a lot of self-soothing with food and drink, perhaps you should concentrate on your other senses. If eating is not a problem for you, try some of these ideas and add some of your own:

☐ Enjoy your favorite foods, savoring every bite and really getting into the taste, texture, temperature, and so on.

☐ Carry a favorite food with you to snack on later in the day.

☐ Eat a juicy piece of fruit, enjoying the cool sweetness.

☐ Drink your favorite beverage, such as coffee or tea. Have it in a special cup or glass and really pay attention to all the sensations of thirst and satisfaction. Don't have anything else with it and don't do anything else while you're drinking.

☐ Have a special treat, like ice cream or candy, once in a while.

☐ Other: _____

☐ Other: _____

☐ Other: _____

Smell

Humans are instinctively drawn to pleasing smells. The sense of smell plays a big role in memory, in appetite, and in sexual attraction. Don't overlook your sense of smell when searching for ways to soothe yourself. You can try these ideas or come up with additional smells you like:

- ☐ Wear perfume or cologne that pleases you.

- ☐ Burn incense or scented candles.

- ☐ Drop by the bakery, florist, or restaurant whose smell you love.

- ☐ Bake cookies or a cake and enjoy the smell that fills your home.

- ☐ Put some fresh flowers on your desk or dining table.

- ☐ Other: _____

- ☐ Other: _____

- ☐ Other: _____

Touch

Your skin is the largest organ in your body, rich in sensitive nerve endings and a powerful source of pleasure. From this list select some ways to pamper your sense of touch and add other ideas of your own:

- ☐ Stretch to loosen your muscles and ease aches and pains. You can do real yoga or runner's stretches, or just experiment with your own moves.

- ☐ Wear your most comfortable clothes—the worn jeans or soft sweatshirt that just feels good.

- ☐ Take a hot bath or cool shower and enjoy the sensations of water on your skin.

- ☐ Carry some worry beads or a small polished stone with you in your purse or pocket, to touch when you feel tense.

- ☐ Have a massage, or just massage your own muscles.

- ☐ Pet your cat or dog. Research shows that contact with animals is very soothing.

- ☐ Other: _____

- ☐ Other: _____

- ☐ Other: _____

Jeanie used self-soothing to counteract her tendency to ruminate about her failed marriage and poor relationship with her ex-husband. She brightened up her studio apartment with colorful prints and some throw pillows in vivid colors and soft fabrics she loved. She hooked up her laptop to her receiver so she could put her favorite music on "shuffle" and have it playing in the background while she fixed dinner or did the laundry or dishes. She swapped her old, scentless shampoo and body wash for products whose smell she liked, and sometimes she burned sandalwood incense. She set up a weekly date with a friend to treat themselves to manicures, movies, or hot fudge sundaes.

Positive Distraction

To keep chronic anxiety going you need to pay regular attention to your worries. Distraction reduces anxiety by turning your attention elsewhere, away from your fears. We call this "positive distraction" to distinguish it from the kind of knee-jerk, desperate, negative, momentary distraction that serves as a safety behavior. Positive distraction involves planning ahead to engage over time with other people in meaningful activities, or to occupy your mind with pleasurable games or productive thoughts such as planning exciting home improvements or a vacation.

Pay Attention to Other People

Volunteer. Serve at the soup kitchen. Visit shut-ins. Stuff envelopes for your favorite non-profit. Collect unwanted items for the community rummage sale. By doing something positive for other people, you will distract yourself from the negative things in your own life.

You don't have to get involved in an organized charity to pay attention to other people. Call up a family member or friend who needs help and offer your assistance. Help your grandma organize her photos. Help Uncle Bill clean out the garage. Babysit while your friend goes to the doctor. Or just have lunch with friends and listen to their problems instead of dwelling on your own.

In fact, you don't even have to know the other people you are using for distraction. Go people-watching at the park or mall. Plant yourself in the middle of a lunch counter and let your awareness of others expand. Eavesdrop on their conversations. Observe how they sit, stand, and walk. Keep a tally of bright or dull colors, kinds of shoes, or hairstyles. If you catch yourself worrying about your own usual problems, refocus on what other people are doing.

You can use photos of other people to distract yourself when you are alone. Carry pictures of people you love or admire. Take them out and look at them for a ready source of distraction.

What other ways can you think of to distract yourself by observing others?

Pay Attention to Other Activities

Tasks and chores can take your mind off your worries. If you're like most people, there are plenty of things in your life that you have been meaning to do, but you never seem to get around to them. Take a moment right now to update your "To Do" list. The next time you find yourself consumed by anxiety, do something on the list as a distraction from worry. Here are some typical items to get you started, and room to add your own tasks:

- ☐ Reorganize your filing system, address book, desktop, etc.
- ☐ Cook a real dinner for yourself or friends.
- ☐ Get a haircut or your nails done.
- ☐ Pay your bills.
- ☐ Wash the dishes.
- ☐ Make a phone call you've been putting off.
- ☐ Write down a plan to get a better job.
- ☐ Fill a box with stuff you don't want and drop it off at the thrift store.
- ☐ Flatten all the cardboard boxes in the recycling.
- ☐ Rearrange the furniture.
- ☐ Really clean up one room.
- ☐ Weed a flower bed or mow the lawn.
- ☐ Cut your toenails.
- ☐ Polish shoes or jewelry.
- ☐ Straighten out a messy drawer or cupboard.
- ☐ Other: _____
- ☐ Other: _____
- ☐ Other: _____

Pay Attention to Other Thoughts

It's hard to stop thinking about your worries because the deliberate attempt to suppress a thought often makes that thought more likely to occur. This mental quirk was studied in the 1980s by social psychologist Daniel Wegner, who called it the "ironic mental process" (1987).

Over a hundred years earlier, Russian novelist Fyodor Dostoevsky put it this way: "Try to pose for yourself this task: not to think of a polar bear, and you will see that the cursed thing will come to mind every minute" (1863). To this day people refer to ironic mental processes as the "white bear problem."

You can escape the white bear problem by consciously choosing to think about other, more interesting things. Here is a list of alternative trains of thought onto which you might jump to avoid the white bear:

- ☐ Recall happier times. Dwell on your experiences in the past that were fun, exciting, or gratifying. What happened when? Who was there? How did events unfold? Go into great detail with all the sense impressions of sights, sounds, smells, and so on.

- ☐ Indulge in sexual fantasies you enjoy. What would you like to do? Who would you like to do it with? Think of as many details as you can.

- ☐ Become the hero of your own story. Reimagine a past experience and edit the scene so that you are the center of the action, the one who pulls off amazing feats, wins the game, saves the day.

- ☐ Imagine that someone you greatly respect is praising you. Listen as this person tells you how smart, important, accomplished, attractive, or special you are.

- ☐ Enjoy a fantasy in which a dream comes true: how you would spend six million dollars, what it would be like to win a gold medal at the Olympics, what you would say when you received the Nobel Peace Prize.

- ☐ If you have a favorite saying, quotation, or prayer, write it out carefully on a small card and carry it with you. When you need to distract yourself from other thoughts, pull out the card and read the inspiring words.

- ☐ Other: _____

- ☐ Other: _____

- ☐ Other: _____

Sandy took her mind off her health and financial troubles by staying busy. She volunteered at the public library, shelving books and pricing paperbacks for the annual book sale. Each week on Sunday morning she cleaned out one drawer or cabinet in her house, sorting things into "keep here," "move there," "throw out," or "donate." When thoughts about her dwindling savings or possible future surgery intruded, she reminded herself to take it "one day at a time," a meaningful saying that she had written on an index card and kept in her purse.

Coping Thoughts

Tolerating distress is largely a mental ability. In this section you will improve your mental distress tolerance by exploring the probabilities that the events you dread might come to pass, and by preparing mental coping statements to use when you do have to get through distressing situations.

Probabilities

If you live in fear of having a panic attack, this is the section for you. It counteracts the two processes that can lead to panic: overestimation and catastrophizing. Overestimation is the tendency to overestimate the odds of bad things happening. For example, the chance of the average driver having an auto accident in any 24-hour period is 0.0015 percent, or about one in ten thousand; however, a panicky person drives as if it were a 60 percent possibility.

Catastrophizing is the tendency to predict that when a bad thing *does* happen it will be a total catastrophe. So a panicky driver will assume that if an accident happens then everyone will die, even though only 1 percent of traffic accidents involve a fatality.

The way to fight panic is to explore your overestimation and catastrophizing and revise your thinking about probabilities. To do that, use the following Probability Worksheet. (A downloadable version of the worksheet is available at http://www.newharbinger.com/34749.) Here are instructions:

Event: In the first column, write down an event that you typically dread. This can be an observable external experience like fainting or vomiting while giving a speech, or a purely internal experience like feeling dizzy or spacey.

Automatic thoughts: In the second column, write down your automatic thoughts about the event. These are the things you say to yourself about what is likely to happen.

Probability: In the third column put a percentage from 0 to 100 percent, according to how likely it seems that the dreaded event will occur. Zero percent means that there is no chance of experiencing the event, and 100 percent means that the feared event will inevitably happen.

Anxiety: As you imagine experiencing what you fear, in the next column rate your level of anxiety in the same way, from 0 to 100 percent, with 100 percent being the worst anxiety you have ever felt.

Evidence pro and con: In this column write down whatever evidence you can think of to support or contradict your automatic thoughts. Ask yourself these questions:

- In all the times I've feared this happening, how many times has it actually happened?

- When it didn't happen, what happened instead?

- Have I had any outcomes in the past that were better than I feared?

- What actual facts about this event do I know? (statistics, medical realities, observations)

- How long is the feared event likely to last? Can I tolerate it that long?

Coping alternatives: In this column describe what you can do if the event occurs. Include things like the breath exercises in this chapter, family or friends you can call on for help, coping skills you've used in the past, strategies you've seen others use successfully, and so on.

Probability and anxiety: Finally, in the last two columns re-rate your estimate of the probability of the occurrence and your anxiety level now, after reviewing the evidence pro and con and your coping alternatives.

Probability Worksheet

Event	Automatic thoughts	Probability 0–100%	Anxiety 0–100%	Evidence pro and con	Coping alternatives	Probability 0–100%	Anxiety 0–100%

How did you do? Hopefully the process of weighing the evidence and your coping alternatives accomplished two goals: helping you estimate risk more accurately and increasing your confidence in your ability to cope.

Here is how Juan filled out his Probability Worksheet to process his fears about his daughter's safety:

Juan's Probability Worksheet

Event	Automatic thoughts	Probability 0–100%	Anxiety 0–100%	Evidence pro and con	Coping alternatives	Probability 0–100%	Anxiety 0–100%
My daughter Angela will get mugged and raped	She's so vulnerable, it's bound to happen	90%	95%	Pro: it happened to her mother, this is a dangerous neighborhood. Con: she's careful, doesn't walk alone at night, we have Neighborhood Watch now.	Her mother survived it, there is less stigma and more counseling these days, she has loving parents.	35%	45%

Cognitive Coping Statements

To prepare for the events you dread, prepare cognitive coping statements ahead of time. These are short mental affirmations that perform many important functions in regulating anxiety. They remind you that you have coping alternatives, that there is no need to panic, and that you can relax away any stress you feel. Your coping statements should say that catastrophic fear is not valid and provide a realistic estimate of the worst that could happen. Finally, these statements can help you lower unreasonably high expectations and focus on meeting the challenges of difficult situations. Here are some examples of good cognitive coping statements:

- I can always pause for a moment and take a deep breath to relax.

- Feeling nervous is normal; no need to panic about it.

- I've survived this before. Just breathe and get through it.

- At the very worst, it will be over soon.

- I know my stuff.

- I'll do my best and that will be good enough.

Now try composing some cognitive coping statement for yourself:

_____

_____

_____

_____

_____

In this chapter you have learned five different ways to build up your tolerance for anxiety, starting with mindfulness and relaxation exercises to aid you in feeling calmer when you need to. The suggestions for self-soothing and distraction can help in forming positive new habits and making lifestyle changes that will make anxiety a smaller and less constricting part of your daily life. Finally, your increased skill in formulating coping thoughts will get you through unavoidable stressful situations with less anxiety.

Please keep in mind that the distress tolerance techniques in this chapter should not be used while you are doing the exposure exercises in the earlier chapters. In exposure treatment, the goal is to actually experience the full range of emotions. Practicing distress tolerance at the same time will make exposure less effective.

CHAPTER 11

Relapse Prevention

When you're talking about anxiety, relapse is not actually "preventable," in the sense that it will never happen again. The occasional feeling of anxiety is an inevitable fact of life. You are bound to feel anxious again, probably sooner rather than later. But if you face your fears and carry on with your chosen path in life in spite of your anxiety, that's not really a relapse in the terms of this chapter.

However, if you fall back into your old patterns of avoidance and allow anxiety to divert you from what you want to do in life, that *is* the kind of relapse we're talking about in this chapter. And let's be honest: that kind of relapse is also a fact of life, because no change is perfectly straightforward. In the real world, psychological change happens in a stop-and-start, back-and-forth fashion. You take two or three steps forward, then a step or two backward. It's like driving a manual shift car up a hill in heavy traffic. Periodically, traffic stops your forward momentum and you have to brake, push in the clutch, downshift, and then try to get going again. Typically, you have to roll backward a little bit before you get the gas and clutch coordinated and start going forward again. The key is to not stall the engine, not stop too long, and not roll so far backward that you have a fender bender.

To switch metaphors, let's compare emotional health to physical health. It would be nice if anxiety could be treated the way we treat some physical problems. If you could have your anxiety surgically removed like a bad appendix, that would be great. But it doesn't work that way. Fixing emotional problems is more like renewing your tetanus shot every few years or developing the habit of applying sunscreen before you go out. You have to keep treating the problem. The emotional skills you've learned in this chapter have to be renewed or reapplied from time to time, so consider the skills you have learned in this book to be something you have on hand, to use as needed when you relapse into avoiding what you fear.

If you find yourself relapsing into prolonged anxiety and avoidance, remember that's natural. It happens to everybody. It's the signal that you need to apply the plan you made in this chapter, to apply your emotional sunscreen, step on the gas, let out the clutch, and resume your journey.

How Relapse Happens

For perhaps the first time in your life you have accepted and endured your anxiety by exposing yourself to a feared situation that you formerly avoided. And you got through it okay. You didn't die, didn't melt down, didn't explode or blow away in the wind. This success gives you a rush of very pleasant self-confidence and pride. It can be a high, even an altered state. Brain chemicals called endorphins flood your neurons like a runner who has just crossed the finish line at the head of the pack.

But eventually the endorphins of successful change are reabsorbed. Your brain chemistry literally changes and the thrill is gone, the honeymoon is over. Along comes a stressor, you feel anxious, and old patterns of avoidance reassert themselves. Anxiety starts to feed off itself and spiral upward. The whole process is not only scary, but it's also depressing, because it feels like failure. Your new confidence and self-esteem evaporate.

Making a Relapse Plan

Since relapse is inevitable, it makes sense to plan for it. The first step in crafting a plan is to make a list of alarm bells.

My Alarm Bells

Alarm bells are all the things in your life that can signal the start of a relapse. An appointment in a high-rise building can be an alarm bell if you fear heights. A person such as a police officer or tax auditor can be an alarm bell if you get nervous around authority figures. Certain thoughts or memories can be alarm bells if you can't stop thinking about them. An upcoming meeting on your schedule might be an alarm bell, or it might not be an alarm bell unless you try to postpone it or start obsessively overpreparing for it. Everybody's alarm bells are different.

In the following exercise, make a detailed list of your personal alarm bells. (A downloadable version of this worksheet is available at http://www.newharbinger.com/34749.)

Stressor Alarm Bells

Who (particular people)
What (things, situations)
Where (places)
When (events)

Cognitive Alarm Bells

Thought suppression

Distraction through fantasies, mantras, prayer

Rigid thinking (obsessively repeating the same thoughts)

Prolonged worrying

Misappraisal of threat (overestimating danger)

Sensation Avoidance Alarm Bells

Feeling too hot or cold

Being very tired, exhausted

Getting out of breath, sweaty

Sexual arousal

Safety Behavior Alarm Bells

Excessive reassurance seeking

Distraction

Procrastination

Overpreparation

Checking and double-checking

Rituals

Perfectionism

Overreliance on a support person

- *Example: Allison's Fears*

Allison was a forty-two-year-old physical therapist who was afraid of heights, enclosed spaces, authority figures, and confrontations with her father and ex-husband. She filled out her Alarm Bells lists like this:

Allison's Stressor Alarm Bells

Who (particular people)   *Father, ex-husband*
What (things, situations)   *Evaluations with my supervisor, talking to the lawyers or judge*
Where (places)   *Hospital administration offices, high-rise hotels, steep hiking trail*
When (events)   *Camping with daughter in claustrophobic tent, cliffside trail*

Allison's Cognitive Alarm Bells

Thought suppression
Distraction through fantasies, mantras, prayer
Rigid thinking (obsessively repeating the same thoughts) *I'll never be free of my ex-husband* *My father likes my ex more than me*
Prolonged worrying *When I catch myself staring at the wall, worrying, frozen in place* *Thinking supervisor wants to fire me, hospital administration thinks I'm a malcontent*
Misappraisal of threat (overestimating danger) *Thinking it's inevitable that I'll lose my job and be homeless someday*

Allison's Sensation Avoidance Alarm Bells

Feeling too hot or cold *Camping trip this summer*
Being very tired, exhausted
Getting out of breath, sweaty *Hiking with my daughter*
Sexual arousal

Allison's Safety Behavior Alarm Bells

Excessive reassurance seeking
Pestering my daughter about snakes, poison ivy, first aid kits
Distraction
Playing games on my phone when I should be taking care of business
Procrastination
Being late with papers that need to be signed
Overpreparation
More than two drafts of an equipment request
Spending more than an hour on case notes
Checking and double-checking
Rituals
Perfectionism
See "Overpreparation"
Overreliance on a support person

My Relapse Plan

When one or more of your alarm bells goes off, it's time to apply the skills you've practiced in this book. It is a three-step process:

1. **Name it and claim it.** Don't pretend everything is okay. Go immediately back to the first three chapters of this book, where you learned about the nature of anxiety and assessed how it particularly affects you.

2. **Cut avoidance short.** Use chapters 4, 5, and 6 of this book to figure out how best to expose yourself to your fears and get past them.

3. **Use auxiliary techniques as needed.** Review chapters 7 through 10 for other ways to cope with anxiety in addition to exposure.

• *Example: Allison's Relapse Strategy*

Alarm bells went off for Allison as her daughter Rachael's school camping trip approached. Twice, Allison almost "accidentally" signed up for extra physical therapy hours at the hospital on the same weekend as the camping trip. She annoyed her daughter by repeatedly quizzing her about such things as the likelihood of rattlesnakes or polluted stream water.

"Mom," Rachael said, "if you don't want to go, I wish you'd just say it."

"No, no, I want to go," Allison lied. She realized that her alarm bells were ringing loud and clear and that she was on the verge of backing out of the trip, which would have deeply disappointed her daughter. She needed to "name it and claim it" before she relapsed completely and avoided the trip entirely.

Allison stopped her safety behavior of asking for reassurance, and blocked out the weekend clearly on her calendars at work and at home. When the dreaded weekend arrived, she loaded the car and set off with Rachael on time, biting her tongue to stop herself from worrying out loud. In the mountains she drank the water, slept in the dark and confining tent, and hiked up the scary trail to the waterfall. She felt anxious several times during the weekend, but the feelings soon passed. Overall, she had a good time, especially when Rachael said that camping together was "the best."

A couple of months later, Allison had to receive an evaluation from her supervisor. She caught herself ruminating furiously about the upcoming meeting, when there was nothing she could do about it. She wanted to call in sick, maybe even quit, to avoid her supervisor, but she didn't. She fell back on her defusion skills from chapter 8, telling herself, "There's a 'getting fired' thought again" and "Thank you, mind, for that inadequacy thought." Her anxiety relaxed a little and she got through the evaluation with her job intact. In fact, her supervisor remarked, "You haven't seemed so nervous lately."

Allison's father and ex-husband were involved in a family business, so her divorce was a nightmare of recriminations, bad feelings, and complex negotiations. She was supposed to read and sign a thick stack of papers that sat on her nightstand for two weeks past the date by which she had promised to return them. She moved them to the dining room table to work on them, then distracted herself by binge-watching TV until the papers were covered with junk mail and she forgot where she had put them. One day she was playing a game on her phone when yet another text from her ex-husband reminded her that she was avoiding signing the papers. She realized that her procrastination and distraction behaviors were alarm bells. She turned off her phone right then, ransacked the house until she found the papers, and forced herself to sit in a straight chair at the dining room table until she had read and signed them all. It took a painful two hours, but she was relieved when she was finally done.

A Contract with Yourself

Summarize your relapse plan by using the following worksheet to make a contract with yourself. Even though you have already listed your alarm bells in the previous exercise, it's a good idea to refine that list here to reinforce your plan. (A downloadable version of this contract is available at http://www.newharbinger.com/34749.)

Contract

When these alarm bells ring:

_____

_____

_____

_____

_____

_____

I will:

1. Name it a relapse and claim responsibility for it.

2. Confront, encounter, and expose myself to what I fear, cutting avoidance short.

3. Handle my stressors with my auxiliary skills of cognitive flexibility, defusion, accurate threat assessment, and distress tolerance.

Signature _____ Date _____

- ## *Example: Allison's Contract*

Here is Allison's contract with herself:

Contract

When these alarm bells ring:

Scary trip with daughter

Business meeting with ex-husband

Avoiding entering a high building

Being evaluated or judged by others

Overpreparing for stressful work meetings

Constant worry

I will:

1. Name it a relapse and claim responsibility for it.

2. Confront, encounter, and expose myself to what I fear, cutting avoidance short.

3. Handle my stressors with my auxiliary skills of cognitive flexibility, defusion, accurate threat assessment, and distress tolerance.

Signature ____*Allison*____   Date ____*April 23*____

Going Forward

You've come a long way in your journey through this book. Congratulations on your persistence and your dedication to living your life according to your true values, in spite of your fears. As you go forward and encounter challenges from day to day, remember that although some relapse is inevitable, you have a plan to get back on track, and the skills to accomplish it.

APPENDIX I

Comprehensive Coping Inventory (CCI)

The Comprehensive Coping Inventory (CCI) is here in the appendix so it can be easily reproduced. The CCI was used in chapter 2 to assess your use of four maladaptive coping mechanisms:

Avoidance of danger—the foremost safety behavior

Worry or rumination about danger

Misappraisal or overestimation of danger

Underestimation of your ability to cope with danger

Each of the four subscales of the CCI targets one of the four causes and maintaining factors of anxiety. You are encouraged to take the inventory several times during this treatment program so you can recognize progress, as well as what still needs work.

Comprehensive Coping Inventory

The items in this inventory are different ways of dealing with problems. As you complete this inventory, think about difficult or stressful events in your life. Do your best to rate each item in terms of how frequently you use it. There are no right or wrong answers, so choose the most accurate answer for you, not what you think is most acceptable, or what most people would say or do.

Rate each item on a scale of 1 to 5, where 1 means you don't use that strategy at all, and 5 means you use it a great deal.

_____ 1.1　I try to stay away from things that make me anxious or uncomfortable rather than face them.

_____ 1.2　I worry about all the bad things that could happen in the future.

_____ 1.3　When I get upset by a situation, my negative thoughts often don't turn out to be completely true.

_____ 1.4　I don't believe I can cope with situations in which I feel anxious or fearful.

_____ 2.1　I tend to avoid situations, people, places, or things that make me feel anxious or upset.

_____ 2.2　I tend to focus on all the negative outcomes that might result from a decision.

_____ 2.3　I tend to assume things will be worse—more painful and scary—than they turn out to be.

_____ 2.4　I doubt my ability to face situations that trigger anxiety.

_____ 3.1　If I feel anxious and uncomfortable I avoid situations altogether—even though I wish I didn't have to.

_____ 3.2　Whenever there's a problem, I tend to dwell on the worst things that could happen.

_____ 3.3　When the situations are especially upsetting to me, I tend to have a string of thoughts about myself or others that feel true at the time, but often aren't.

_____ 3.4　I don't know how to cope with anxious feelings or situations in which I am fearful.

_____ 4.1   There are situations or things that make me anxious, and I try to avoid them.

_____ 4.2   I find that I tend to overthink bad scenarios that could happen.

_____ 4.3   I easily jump to conclusions when I'm upset by something—and my conclusions aren't really accurate.

_____ 4.4   I feel distressed by fear or anxiety in a way that seems too big to cope with.

_____ 5.1   I try to avoid things I feel I must do to protect myself from feeling too anxious.

_____ 5.2   My problems trigger a lot of thinking about all the bad directions things could take.

_____ 5.3   In difficult situations I can have one negative thought after another that makes things seem worse than they really are.

_____ 5.4   I don't feel strong enough to face fear-inducing situations.

You might feel overwhelmed by the number of items that were relevant for you. The good news is that you are bringing awareness to the coping behaviors that are reinforcing your anxiety. This is where the change starts to happen.

Let's look at what's significant for you.

1.1, 2.1, 3.1, 4.1, and 5.1 are statements that apply to _avoidance_ of the things that make you feel anxious. These can be people, places, situations, things, or internal sensations that you tend to avoid.

1.2, 2.2, 3.2, 4.2, and 5.2 are statements that apply to _worry/rumination_, extended worrying about future dangers or threats and making negative predictions about the future that get in the way of creating solutions to problems.

1.3, 2.3, 3.3, 4.3, and 5.3 are statements that apply to _cognitive misappraisal_, evaluating a situation, object, sensation, or person as dangerous when it isn't.

1.4, 2.4, 3.4, 4.4, and 5.4 are statements that apply to _distress intolerance_, the belief that you can't stand certain experiences and the emotions they trigger.

APPENDIX II

Worksheets

All the worksheets for *The CBT Anxiety Solution Workbook* program are gathered here so they can be easily reproduced, and so that you can see the key elements of treatment in one place.

Comprehensive Coping Inventory	186
Exposure Inventory Worksheet	188
Cost of Avoidance Worksheet	189
Values Worksheet	190
Exposure Inventory Worksheet	191
Results Tracker	192
Learning Coping from Exposure Worksheet	193
My Coping Thoughts for Facing Challenging Situations	194
Coping Plan Worksheet	195
Thought Log	196
Predictions Log	197
Problem Continuum Worksheet	198
Probability Worksheet	199
Stressor Alarm Bells	200
Cognitive Alarm Bells	201
Sensation Avoidance Alarm Bells	202
Safety Behavior Alarm Bells	203

Comprehensive Coping Inventory

The items in this inventory are different ways of dealing with problems. As you complete this inventory, think about difficult or stressful events in your life. Do your best to rate each item in terms of how frequently you use it. There are no right or wrong answers, so choose the most accurate answer for you, not what you think is most acceptable, or what most people would say or do.

Rate each item on a scale of 1 to 5, where 1 means you don't use that strategy at all, and 5 means you use it a great deal.

_____ 1.1   I try to stay away from things that make me anxious or uncomfortable rather than face them.

_____ 1.2   I worry about all the bad things that could happen in the future.

_____ 1.3   When I get upset by a situation, my negative thoughts often don't turn out to be completely true.

_____ 1.4   I don't believe I can cope with situations in which I feel anxious or fearful.

_____ 2.1   I tend to avoid situations, people, places, or things that make me feel anxious or upset.

_____ 2.2   I tend to focus on all the negative outcomes that might result from a decision.

_____ 2.3   I tend to assume things will be worse—more painful and scary—than they turn out to be.

_____ 2.4   I doubt my ability to face situations that trigger anxiety.

_____ 3.1   If I feel anxious and uncomfortable I avoid situations altogether—even though I wish I didn't have to.

_____ 3.2   Whenever there's a problem, I tend to dwell on the worst things that could happen.

_____ 3.3   When the situations are especially upsetting to me, I tend to have a string of thoughts about myself or others that feel true at the time, but often aren't.

_____ 3.4   I don't know how to cope with anxious feelings or situations in which I am fearful.

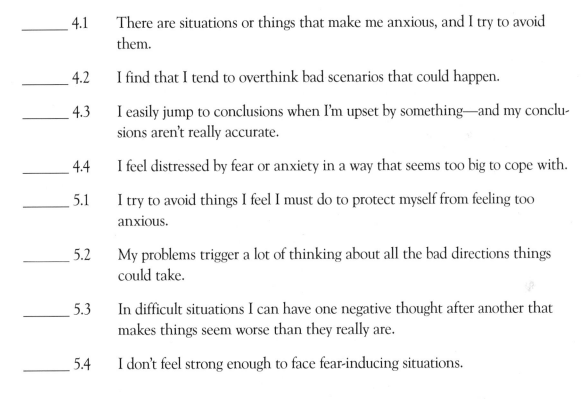

_____ 4.1   There are situations or things that make me anxious, and I try to avoid them.

_____ 4.2   I find that I tend to overthink bad scenarios that could happen.

_____ 4.3   I easily jump to conclusions when I'm upset by something—and my conclusions aren't really accurate.

_____ 4.4   I feel distressed by fear or anxiety in a way that seems too big to cope with.

_____ 5.1   I try to avoid things I feel I must do to protect myself from feeling too anxious.

_____ 5.2   My problems trigger a lot of thinking about all the bad directions things could take.

_____ 5.3   In difficult situations I can have one negative thought after another that makes things seem worse than they really are.

_____ 5.4   I don't feel strong enough to face fear-inducing situations.

You might feel overwhelmed by the number of items that were relevant for you. The good news is that you are bringing awareness to the coping behaviors that are reinforcing your anxiety. This is where the change starts to happen. Let's look at what's significant for you.

1.1, 2.1, 3.1, 4.1, and 5.1 are statements that apply to *avoidance* of the things that make you feel anxious. These can be people, places, situations, things, or internal sensations that you tend to avoid.

1.2, 2.2, 3.2, 4.2, and 5.2 are statements that apply to *worry/rumination*, extended worrying about future dangers or threats and making negative predictions about the future that get in the way of creating solutions to problems.

1.3, 2.3, 3.3, 4.3, and 5.3 are statements that apply to *cognitive misappraisal*, evaluating a situation, object, sensation, or person as dangerous when it isn't.

1.4, 2.4, 3.4, 4.4, and 5.4 are statements that apply to *distress intolerance*, the belief that you can't stand certain experiences and the emotions they trigger.

Exposure Inventory Worksheet

Feared situation	SUDS 0–100	Safety behaviors

Cost of Avoidance Worksheet

Domain	Avoidance or other safety behaviors	Negative impact on my life	Rating 1–5
Friendships			
Family			
Parenting			
Work/education			
Self-care/health			
Pleasure, recreation, social activities			
Life goals			
Service to others			
Romantic relationships			

Values Worksheet

Fear (Things I avoid)	Blocked valued activities	Values rating 1–5

Exposure Inventory Worksheet

Feared situation	Safety behaviors	Plan to stop safety behavior and to expose	SUDS 1–100	Value 1–5	Predicted worst-case outcome	Percent probability

Results Tracker

Exposure:

Predicted worst-case outcome:

1. Did the worst-case outcome happen? _____ Yes _____ No

2. What happened instead?

3. Percent probability: Before: _____ After: _____

4. What did you learn from the exposure?

5. SUDS 1–100: Before: _____ After: _____

Learning Coping from Exposure Worksheet

Exposure experience	SUDS: Before	How I coped	SUDS: After

My Coping Thoughts for Facing Challenging Situations

My coping thoughts for facing challenging situations

My coping thoughts for facing fear itself

Coping Plan Worksheet

Worst-case scenario: _____

_____

_____

_____

Behavioral coping: _____

_____

_____

_____

Emotional coping: _____

_____

_____

_____

Cognitive coping: _____

_____

_____

_____

Interpersonal coping: _____

_____

_____

_____

Thought Log

Thought	Negative prediction	Negative focus	Problem magnification

Predictions Log

Predictions (What terrible thing will happen and when)	What actually occurred

Problem Continuum Worksheet

Problems	Problem continuum	
	(Rank big to small)	Your problems
A terminal diagnosis	_____	_____
Death of a loved one	_____	_____
Loss of your job	_____	_____
House foreclosure	_____	_____
Divorce/breakup	_____	_____
Mild criticism from your boss	_____	_____
Mild disagreement with a friend	_____	_____
Loss of your wallet	_____	_____
A big auto repair bill	_____	_____
Car breakdown—need to be towed	_____	_____
Refrigerator needs replacing	_____	_____
Late for work	_____	_____

Probability Worksheet

Event	Automatic thoughts	Probability 0–100%	Anxiety 0–100%	Evidence pro and con	Coping alternatives	Probability 0–100%	Anxiety 0–100%

Stressor Alarm Bells

Who (particular people)

What (things, situations)

Where (places)

When (events)

Cognitive Alarm Bells

Thought suppression

Distraction through fantasies, mantras, prayer

Rigid thinking (obsessively repeating the same thoughts)

Prolonged worrying

Misappraisal of threat (overestimating danger)

Sensation Avoidance Alarm Bells

Feeling too hot or cold

Being very tired, exhausted

Getting out of breath, sweaty

Sexual arousal

Safety Behavior Alarm Bells

Excessive reassurance seeking

Distraction

Procrastination

Overpreparation

Checking and double-checking

Rituals

Perfectionism

Overreliance on a support person

Contract

When these alarm bells ring:

_____

_____

_____

_____

_____

_____

I will:

1. Name it a relapse and claim responsibility for it.

2. Confront, encounter, and expose myself to what I fear, cutting avoidance short.

3. Handle my stressors with my auxiliary skills of cognitive flexibility, defusion, accurate threat assessment, and distress tolerance.

Signature _____ Date _____

Depression Anxiety Stress Scales-21 (DASS-21)

This widely used questionnaire allows you to identify your levels of depression, anxiety, and stress. Norms are provided so you can see how your scores rate in terms of severity. This is a repeatable measure, meaning you can take it over and over. You are encouraged to take the DASS-21 several times throughout the treatment program to assess your progress.

DASS-21

Name: _____	Date: _____

Please read each statement and circle a number (0, 1, 2, or 3) that indicates how much the statement applied to you *over the past week*. There are no right or wrong answers. Do not spend too much time on any statement.

The rating scale is as follows:

0   Did not apply to me at all

1   Applied to me to some degree, or some of the time

2   Applied to me to a considerable degree, or a good part of the time

3   Applied to me very much, or most of the time

1	I was aware of dryness of my mouth.	0 1 2 3
2	I experienced breathing difficulty (e.g., excessively rapid breathing, breathlessness in the absence of physical exertion).	0 1 2 3
3	I experienced trembling (e.g., in the hands).	0 1 2 3
4	I was worried about situations in which I might panic and make a fool of myself.	0 1 2 3
5	I felt I was close to panic.	0 1 2 3
6	I was aware of the action of my heart in the absence of physical exertion (e.g., sense of heart rate increase, heart missing a beat).	0 1 2 3
7	I felt scared without any good reason.	0 1 2 3

Scoring: Add up your scores for all items and compare to the table of anxiety norms below:

0–7	Normal
8–9	Mild anxiety
10–14	Moderate anxiety
15–19	Severe anxiety
20+	Extremely severe anxiety

Interoceptive Exposure

Interoceptive exposure[*] involves using exercises that reproduce or mimic body sensations associated with panic, such as rapid heartbeat, shortness of breath, feeling hot or flushed, dizziness or lightheadedness, or shakiness and weakness in your legs. Because people who struggle with panic come to fear these sensations, overcoming panic disorder involves exposing themselves to these very same sensations.

Included here is a full range of exercises typically used for interoceptive exposure. You can briefly try them all, and then fully expose yourself to the exercises that feel most similar to your own panic sensations.

Interoceptive Desensitization

Interoceptive desensitization is among the most effective—and challenging—components of the treatment program for panic disorder. What you're about to do is recreate, in a safe way, bodily sensations similar to those you associate with panic. You can learn to experience these sensations as something uncomfortable but not frightening. Dizziness, rapid heartbeat, even feelings of unreality can become no more than annoying effects of the fight-or-flight response. And when these feelings are no longer associated with panic, you'll find yourself less vigilant toward, and less focused on, the sensations inside your body.

Desensitizing to frightening bodily sensations is accomplished in three stages. In the first stage you briefly expose yourself to ten specific sensations and then rate your reactions. Most of the following exposure exercises were developed and tested by Michelle Craske and David Barlow (2007). They induce feelings similar to those many people report prior to or during a panic.

---

[*] Reprinted with permission from McKay, Davis, and Fanning, 2011, *Thoughts and Feelings: Taking Control of Your Moods and Your Life.*

- Shaking your head from side to side

- Lowering your head between your legs, then lifting it

- Running in place (check with your doctor first)

- Running in place wearing a heavy jacket

- Holding your breath

- Tensing the major muscles—particularly in your abdomen

- Spinning while you sit in a swivel chair (not to be done standing up)

- Breathing very rapidly

- Breathing through a single, narrow straw

- Staring at yourself in a mirror

As you review this list, you can probably already tell that some of these sensations will be quite uncomfortable. But it is precisely the feelings you most fear that you must desensitize to in order to recover from panic disorder. If exposing yourself to these interoceptive (physically arousing) experiences feels too frightening to do alone, enlist a support person to be present throughout the exercise. Later you can discontinue support as you get more comfortable with the sensations.

When you expose yourself to each of the ten sensations, you'll need to keep records to identify which ones create the most anxiety and have the greatest similarity to your panic feelings. Fill in the Interoceptive Assessment Chart that follows as you sequentially expose yourself to each interoceptive experience.

Interoceptive Assessment Chart

Exercise	Duration	Anxiety 0–100	Similarity to panic sensations 0–100%
Shaking head from side to side	30 seconds		
Lowering your head between your legs, then lifting it (keep repeating)	30 seconds		
Running in place	60 seconds		
Running in place wearing a heavy jacket	60 seconds		
Holding your breath	30 seconds (or as long as you can)		
Tensing the major muscles—particularly in your abdomen	60 seconds (or as long as you can)		
Spinning while you sit in a swivel chair	60 seconds		
Breathing very rapidly	Up to 60 seconds		
Breathing through a single narrow straw	120 seconds		
Staring at yourself in a mirror	90 seconds		

When rating your anxiety intensity, the scale ranges from 0 to 100, where 100 is the worst anxiety you've ever felt. The column where you rate each exercise's similarity to panic sensations is very important. The range is from 0 percent similarity to 100 percent—absolutely identical feelings.

Stage 2 of interoceptive desensitization involves making a hierarchy of frightening sensations from the Interoceptive Assessment Chart. Here's what you do: Put a check by each exercise that you rated 40 percent or above in similarity to actual panic sensations. Now, on the Interoceptive Hierarchy/Anxiety Intensity Chart, rank the *checked* exercises from the least to the greatest anxiety-intensity rating. Fill in the anxiety rating from your first exposure under Trial 1.

Interoceptive Hierarchy/Anxiety Intensity Chart

Exercise	Trial 1	Trial 2	Trial 3	Trial 4	Trial 5	Trial 6	Trial 7	Trial 8
1.								
2.								
3.								
4.								
5.								
6.								
7.								
8.								
9.								
10.								

Once you've developed your hierarchy, it's time to begin stage 3—the actual desensitization process. Start with the item lowest in anxiety on your hierarchy chart. If you need to have a support person present during initial exposure, that's fine. Here's the actual desensitization sequence:

1. Begin the exercise and note the point where you first experience uncomfortable sensations. Stick with the exercise at least thirty seconds *after* the onset of uncomfortable sensations—the longer the better.

2. As soon as you stop the exercise, rate your anxiety in the box for each exposure trial (on your Interoceptive Hierarchy/Anxiety Intensity Chart).

3. Immediately following each exercise, begin controlled breathing.

4. Following each exercise, remind yourself of the medical realities relevant to the bodily sensations you're experiencing. For example, if you feel light-headed or dizzy after rapid breathing, remind yourself that this is a temporary and harmless sensation caused by reduced oxygen to the brain. Or, if you have a rapid heart rate after running in place, you could remind yourself that a healthy heart can beat 200 times a minute for weeks without damage, and it's certainly built to handle this little bit of exercise.

5. Continue trials of desensitization with each exercise until your anxiety rating is no more than 25.

Sample Interoceptive Hierarchy/Anxiety Intensity Chart

Exercise	Trial 1	Trial 2	Trial 3	Trial 4	Trial 5	Trial 6	Trial 7	Trial 8
1. *Staring in the mirror*	40							
2. Holding breath	45							
3. Breathing through straw	50							
4. Running in place	60							
5. Running wearing jacket	70							
6. Breathing rapidly	80							
7.								
8.								
9.								
10.								

Interoceptive Desensitization in Natural Settings

When you've worked through your hierarchy to the point where each exercise triggers an anxiety-intensity rating of no more than 25, you can begin desensitization in real-life settings. With medical clearance, you can begin exposure to activities and experiences you've avoided because you feared a panic attack. Make a list of these activities and arrange them on the Interoceptive Hierarchy/Anxiety Intensity Chart. Rank them from least anxiety-evoking to most.

Acceptance and Action Questionnaire (AAQ-II)

The Acceptance and Action Questionnaire (AAQ-II) is a measure of acceptance versus avoidance. You are encouraged to fill out the questionnaire in the beginning, around the middle, and at the end of your exposure work. Scores should change as your level of avoidance goes down.

AAQ II—Acceptance and Action Questionnaire: A Measure of Your Level of Avoidance

Below you will find a list of statements. Please rate how true each statement is for you by circling a number next to it. Use the scale below to make your choice.

1	2	3	4	5	6	7
never true	very seldom true	seldom true	sometimes true	frequently true	almost always true	always true

1. My painful experiences and memories make it difficult for me to live a life that I would value.
   1 2 3 4 5 6 7

2. I'm afraid of my feelings.
   1 2 3 4 5 6 7

3. I worry about not being able to control my worries and feelings.
   1 2 3 4 5 6 7

4. My painful memories prevent me from having a fulfilling life.
   1 2 3 4 5 6 7

5. Emotions cause problems in my life.
   1 2 3 4 5 6 7

6. It seems like most people are handling their lives better than I am.
   1 2 3 4 5 6 7

7. Worries get in the way of my success.
   1 2 3 4 5 6 7

This is a one-factor measure of experiential avoidance. Score the scale by adding up the scores for the seven items. Higher scores equal greater levels of experiential avoidance.

Bond, F. W., S. C. Hayes, R. A. Baer, K. M. Carpenter, N. Guenole, H. K. Orcutt, T. Waltz, and R. D. Zettle. (2011). "Preliminary psychometric properties of the Acceptance and Action Questionnaire-II: A revised measure of psychological inflexibility and experiential avoidance. *Behavior Therapy*, 42(4): 676-88.

References

Cannon, W. 1915. *Body Changes in Pain, Hunger, Fear, and Rage: An Account of Recent Researches into the Function of Emotional Excitement.* New York: Appleton.

Clark, T. 2011. *Nerve: Poise Under Pressure, Serenity Under Stress, and the Brave New Science of Fear and Cool.* New York: Little Brown & Co.

Craske, M. and D. Barlow. 2007. *Mastery of Your Anxiety and Panic.* New York: Oxford University Press.

Craske, M., M. Treanor, C. Conway, T. Zbozinek, and B. Vervliet. 2014. "Maximizing exposure therapy: An inhibitory learning approach." *Behavior Research and Therapy*, 58, 10–23.

Dostoevsky, F. 1863. "Winter Notes on Summer Impressions." In *Notes from Underground and the Double.* New York: Penguin Classics, 2009.

Hayes, S. C., and K. G. Wilson. 2003. "Mindfulness: Method and process." *Clinical Psychology: Science and Practice*, 10, 161–165.

Linehan, M. M. 1993. *Cognitive Behavioral Treatment of Borderline Personality Disorder.* New York: Guilford Press.

McKay, M., M. Davis, and P. Fanning. 2011. *Thoughts and Feelings: Taking Control of Your Moods and Your Life.* 4th ed. Oakland: New Harbinger Publications.

McKay, M., P. Ona, and P. Fanning. 2011. *Mind and Emotions: A Universal Treatment for Emotional Disorders.* Oakland: New Harbinger Publications.

Wegner, D. M., D. J. Schneider, S. R. Carter, and T. L. White. 1987. "Paradoxical effects of thought suppression." *Journal of Personality and Social Psychology*, 53: 5–13.

Matthew McKay, PhD, is a professor at the Wright Institute in Berkeley, CA. He has authored and coauthored numerous books, including *The Relaxation and Stress Reduction Workbook*, *Self-Esteem*, *Thoughts and Feelings*, *When Anger Hurts*, and *ACT on Life Not on Anger*. McKay received his PhD in clinical psychology from the California School of Professional Psychology, and specializes in the cognitive behavioral treatment of anxiety and depression. He lives and works in the greater San Francisco Bay Area.

Michelle Skeen, PsyD, is a therapist who lives and works in San Francisco, CA. She helps individuals overcome fear-based beliefs utilizing schema awareness, self-compassion, and behavioral- and mindfulness-based approaches. She is author of *Love Me, Don't Leave Me* and coauthor of *Communication Skills for Teens*. Skeen hosts a weekly radio show called *Relationships 2.0 with Dr. Michelle Skeen*. To find out more, visit her website at www.michelleskeen.com.

Patrick Fanning is a professional writer in the mental health field, and founder of a men's support group in Northern California. He has authored and coauthored eight self-help books, including *Self-Esteem*, *Thoughts and Feelings*, *Couple Skills*, and *Mind and Emotions*.

FROM OUR PUBLISHER—

As the publisher at New Harbinger and a clinical psychologist since 1978, I know that emotional problems are best helped with evidence-based therapies. These are the treatments derived from scientific research (randomized controlled trials) that show what works. Whether these treatments are delivered by trained clinicians or found in a self-help book, they are designed to provide you with proven strategies to overcome your problem.

Therapies that aren't evidence-based—whether offered by clinicians or in books—are much less likely to help. In fact, therapies that aren't guided by science may not help you at all. That's why this New Harbinger book is based on scientific evidence that the treatment can relieve emotional pain.

This is important: if this book isn't enough, and you need the help of a skilled therapist, use the following resources to find a clinician trained in the evidence-based protocols appropriate for your problem. And if you need more support—a community that understands what you're going through and can show you ways to cope—resources for that are provided below, as well.

Real help is available for the problems you have been struggling with. The skills you can learn from evidence-based therapies will change your life.

Matthew McKay, PhD
Publisher, New Harbinger Publications

**If you need a therapist, the following organization
can help you find a therapist trained in cognitive behavioral therapy (CBT).**

The Association for Behavioral & Cognitive Therapies (ABCT) Find-a-Therapist service offers a list of therapists schooled in CBT techniques. Therapists listed are licensed professionals who have met the membership requirements of ABCT and who have chosen to appear in the directory.

Please visit www.abct.org and click on *Find a Therapist*.

**For additional support for patients, family, and friends,
please contact the following:**

Anxiety and Depression Association of American (ADAA)
please visit www.adaa.org

National Alliance on Mental Illness (NAMI)
please visit www.nami.org

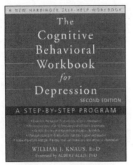

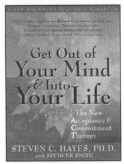

Register your **new harbinger** titles for additional benefits!

When you register your **new harbinger** title—purchased in any format, from any source—you get access to benefits like the following:

- Downloadable accessories like printable worksheets and extra content

- Instructional videos and audio files

- Information about updates, corrections, and new editions

Not every title has accessories, but we're adding new material all the time.

Access free accessories in 3 easy steps:

1. Sign in at NewHarbinger.com (or **register** to create an account).

2. Click on **register a book**. Search for your title and click the **register** button when it appears.

3. Click on the **book cover or title** to go to its details page. Click on **accessories** to view and access files.

That's all there is to it!

If you need help, visit:

NewHarbinger.com/accessories

new harbinger
CELEBRATING
40 YEARS